THE BUS TRIP

Success is a Choice!

A Sports Leadership Fable

Jamy Bechler
Author of *The Leadership Playbook*

D1414203

Copyright © 2019 by Jamy Bechler
www.JamyBechler.com

All rights reserved. No part of this publication may be reproduced,
stored in a retrieval system, or transmitted, in any form or by any
means, electronic, mechanical, photocopying, recording, or otherwise,
without the prior written permission of the author, except in the case
of brief quotations embodied in critical reviews and certain other
noncommercial uses permitted by copyright law.

For permission requests, write to the publisher, with the subject
"Permission Request", at the email address
Support@MHBookServices.com

This book contains information obtained from authentic and highly
regarded sources. Reasonable efforts have been made to publish
reliable data and information, but the author and publisher cannot
assume responsibility for the validity of all materials or the
consequences of their use.

ISBN: 978-0-9992125-6-1

Team or bulk orders are available by contacting
Support@MHBookServices.com

The Bus Trip is a work of fiction designed to help individuals
understand how to be better teammates and more positive leaders.
Names, characters, businesses, organizations, places, events,
incidents, or locales are the product of the author's imagination or are
used fictiously. Any resemblance to actual persons, living or dead, or
locales is entirely coincidental.

THANK YOU ...

Tristen Foote, Lexis Garcia, Ashley Anderson, Konner Beste, Peyton Booth, Travis Daugherty, Matt Grahn, John Motherwell, Jana Pearson, Scott Rodesiler, Sacha Santimano, Matthew Smith, Jessica Southern, and Reed Sutton for your help with the storylines and editing.

To my parents, Frank and Beth Bechler, for raising me the right way and showing me what true servant leadership was as they made the lives of people around them better.

To all my youth league, high school, and college coaches that worked with me and helped me develop.

To all my assistant coaches and colleagues throughout the years who worked tirelessly to make a difference in the lives of student-athletes. I appreciate all you did to help, encourage, and support me during my coaching career.

To all my players throughout the years that exhibited the qualities in this book whether it was during your playing days or after. I'm proud of so many of you for achieving things you never thought possible and maximizing your potential. Every example in this book was rooted in some real-life inspiration from you guys. Thanks for your hard work and sacrifice throughout the years.

Alena Moody for the cover design.

MH Book Services for formatting and producing the book.

Michael Catt, Dan Hughes, Jason Romano, and Brian Stanchak for the back-cover book endorsement.

My last thank you goes out to Tabitha for your love, support, and encouragement throughout this process. This book would not have been possible without you. I love you.

This book is dedicated to my son Jaylen. My prayer for you is that you will be kind to everyone, have a positive influence on the people around you, and make a difference in the world. You're an awesome son. Daddy loves Jaylen!

CONTENTS

WAKE UP

BEEEEEP! BEEEEEEP! BEEEEEEP!

"Seriously, shut that thing off!" shouted Learie.

The alarm definitely seemed to be way too loud and was going off way too early in the morning. But Jaylen knew that it was the exact time it needed to go off because it was the very time that he set it for.

"Are you deaf? Shut that thing off!"

Learie obviously meant business and wasn't a fan of Jaylen's alarm clock.

Jaylen hit the off button.

"Yeah, it was a little loud wasn't it? But regardless, we need to get up. Game Day, right?!?" Jaylen said as he threw off his blanket and hopped out of bed.

"That's what they say. But it doesn't matter for some of us, remember? Some of us just have the best ticket in the arena. Front row every game, baby!"

"Whatever, Captain."

"Captain of the bench you mean."

Even though Learie had been a highly recruited athlete, he had failed to live up to his potential through the years and was now barely playing even though he was a captain. His position was due more to his status as one of only two seniors on the team, rather than anything he had done to be a good team leader.

On the other hand, even though Jaylen was not a captain, he had earned the respect and admiration of seemingly everyone.

"I just know that we've got to get up now because we didn't give ourselves much time to mess around before we need to be on the bus," said Jaylen.

"Maybe but it's not like it'd be the worst thing in the world to get left behind. Then I could enjoy a day off and not have to put up with another loss and the embarrassment of not playing again."

Learie knew that Jaylen didn't like this kind of talk. As the team's starting point guard, the junior took every loss personally.

"Let's focus on what we need to do today."

"What we need," said Learie. "Is a break from this season."

"We'll all get a break soon enough," said Jaylen shaking his head at his roommate. "But we've still got a month before the season is over and until then, we need to get dressed and head over to the gym. Like it or not, we do have another game today. It might be the same old, same old for some, but this is what we do, like it or not. I, for one, can think of hundreds of worse things to do than getting to play basketball and hang out with friends all day."

And with that Learie and Jaylen got dressed and left the dorm. It had seemed as if they had gone through this routine a million times but little did they know that this day would not be like all the rest.

LOADING UP THE BUS

For more than a decade, Denny Dunn had counted the Eagles when he got on the bus. He loved leaving early if it was possible, but he also wanted to make sure that he didn't leave players behind if they left early.

"I counted ten," proclaimed Coach Dunn. Who are we missing?"

"You're joking, right coach?" asked Drew. "We're missing the usuals."

By the usuals, Drew meant James and Antonio. Those two had a habit of being late for everything. They seemed to operate in a world devoid of time, clocks, or calendars.

"Well, they still have a couple of minutes," said Coach Dunn.

"One of these days they are going to cut it too close and totally miss the bus," said Drew.

"We'll deal with that when it happens. For right now, we're lucky that it hasn't happened yet."

"Even though they're our leading scorers, we've been losing, so maybe it wouldn't be so bad if they finally did cut it too close," said Drew. "Maybe our luck would change."

"Our problems are not because of two players," responded Coach Dunn. "Our struggles this year have gone a little deeper than that."

James and Antonio were both similar players, in terms of their athleticism and their versatility on a basketball court. They were both returning all-conference players. Unfortunately, their playing styles and abilities weren't the only things that they had in common. In addition to being late more often than not, they tended to think the world revolved around them both.

Though Coach Dunn was facing the back of the bus talking with Drew and some of the other players, he knew precisely the moment that James and Antonio boarded the bus.

"Game Day, Baby, what, what!" James announced loudly.

"Giddy up. Let's go. Let's get this show on the road. Time to hoop!" said Antonio as the two seemed to feed off one another.

There was certainly no questioning their enthusiasm. Even amidst a losing streak, they were boisterous and energetic. Many of their teammates silently questioned their motives for being so enthusiastic.

"Good morning, fellas," said Mr. Frank.

"Good morning Mr. Frank," the guys said in unison.

Mr. Frank had been driving the team for years. He had seen Coach Dunn and the Eagles experience a lot of success. Unfortunately, this season had been the most challenging Mr. Frank had observed throughout the years of serving as the Eagles' bus driver.

"You ready to be the best you can be today?" asked Mr. Frank.

"You know it!" said Antonio.

"I hope so," Mr. Frank responded. "Your team needs your leadership today."

"Don't worry about that. We're ready to get after it. They can't stop us. We're getting a win today," James boasted confidently.

"Glad to hear that fellas. But you know I'm not talking about you making shots. Just making shots don't make you a leader and isn't always what your team needs but I'm sure you'll figure it out. Today is a bright beautiful day. Great day for us to count our blessings."

"Mr. Frank, you say that to us every time we get on this bus. Instead of calling you Mr. Frank, we should call you Mr. Rainbows and Butterflies. You're one positive guy," said Antonio.

"I try to be, fellas. There's just too much negativity in this world. I just want to see you fellas be the best you can be. Now, speaking about being the best you can be, you better hustle back to your seats. Now, as you said when you got on the bus a few minutes ago, 'It's time to get this show on the road'. But, then again, you already know it's time to go because when you get on the bus, it's always time to go. Literally."

"Wait, did I detect a little sarcasm there, Mr. Frank?" asked Antonio.

With a smile and in his own little *awwhh shucks* sort of way, Mr. Frank said, "You caught me. My wife says I'm doing better with that but still need to watch myself. Now get on back to your seats. This bus is itching to hit the road."

Coach Dunn moved to the side as James and Antonio walked past, barely acknowledging him.

"Well?" asked Coach Dunn.

"Well, what?" responded Antonio.

"We've been waiting on you guys. Is your time more valuable than ours?"

"We had to grab something to eat. You don't want us to be hungry and not play our best, right Coach?" asked James.

"I don't want you to be hungry and I don't want you to play bad which is why we bring food on the bus for you guys."

"Yeah, except when we get on the bus there is never much food left for us," Antonio pointed out.

"Why do you think that is?" asked Coach Dunn.

Antonio and James just stared at Coach Dunn. They didn't really care what he had to say about this issue and were hoping that the question he just asked was rhetorical. They also hoped he would soon be done talking so they could continue to their seats.

Coach Dunn tried to make his point to the guys, "Maybe if you got on the bus when everyone else got on the bus, there would be food for you instead of your teammates getting seconds and thirds before you slow-pokes decide to get on the bus."

"Maybe, coach, but why don't you just get more food next time? Win-win, right?" replied Antonio.

Coach Dunn tended to be more patient than some other coaches but that was put to the test often when dealing with Antonio and James.

"A real win-win would be you guys arriving when your teammates get here and then everybody gets food, we can leave on time, and you don't have to get lectured by me. Win-win-win! Now please go sit down. We're already running a couple of minutes late. We have to get moving."

With that the two players continued past Coach Dunn, rolling their eyes and joining their teammates as Mr. Frank navigated the bus out of the parking lot.

ARRIVAL

This was the kind of trip that Mr. Frank liked. It was all freeway and there was very little traffic to contend with this morning. They would soon be arriving at their destination.

"We're 30 minutes from the gym," Coach Dunn announced. "Everyone, wake up, get out your scouting reports, and let's go over them one last time before we get to the gym."

Most of the players reached into their backpacks for their scouting reports and starting mindlessly reading through it.

"You know what one of the best things about not playing much is?" Demetrius asked his roommate Bobbi. "Scouting reports don't matter to me. I don't have to stop watching Netflix on my phone when Coach says to go over scouting reports."

"What if I get in foul trouble and coach is desperate and has to put you in?" joked Bobbi. "Won't you need to know what is going on?"

"That's funny. If I get into the game, it's over and it won't matter who's a shooter, who's left-handed, or what kind of screens they do on such-and-such play. When I get into the game, it's pickup basketball. It's AAU. It's intramurals. Whatever you want to call it. But for me, it's 'don't matter time' for Demetrius."

Bobbi just looked at his roommate with a mix of sadness and astonishment.

He thought that he saw a couple of players flash a slight smile at the thought of not having practice the day.

Coach Dunn finished up by saying, "The bus will be rolling out in 45 minutes. Get a quick shower, get dressed, get treatment, whatever you need to do but don't lollygag. I don't want to be here any longer than we need to. Remember to pick up all your tape and trash in the locker room. Now bring it in."

"1, 2, 3, Team" and with one of the weaker sounding huddle breaks one will ever hear, a frustrated Coach Dunn walked out of the locker room.

"No practice tomorrow is just fine with me. I'm so sore," said Drew as he hurriedly dressed and left the locker room with a huge smile on his face.

"He might be sore, but I guess scoring a career-high makes you feel a little better," said James as some of his teammates nodded in agreement.

Over in the corner, Antonio sat with his head in his hands after missing what seemed like a million shots. When he looked up, he looked at his hands wondering if he had oil on them. Not only had he missed nearly shot he'd taken, but he also had a record nine turnovers.

"Keep your head up," said Brandon, one of the co-captains. "You'll do better next time. It was just one bad game. None of us played well."

"Pfffttt. You can't win league MVP if you score two points and have a thousand turnovers!" said Antonio.

"I imagine it's also pretty hard to be the Most Valuable Player if you're on a losing team," Brandon pointed out.

"He got you, dude," said James. "We all shot bad. Quit feeling sorry for yourself. You still probably lead the league in scoring. A few more games like that, though, and I might catch you."

James continued, "Shoot, now that I think about it, Drew might even catch up to you."

"I know you guys don't like missing shots but remember that's not the ultimate goal," Brandon reminded them. "Sure, we all want to score, but winning should be what's important, not your stats."

Brandon took off his ankle tape and threw it into the trash can, addressing the guys one last time.

"Now, as Coach said, let's clean this place up, get on the bus, and get out of here."

PARENT CONFRONTATION

Coach Dunn exited the locker room with the stat sheet in his hands. Though the numbers told an ugly story about today's game, he knew that the answers to the team's season-long woes were not contained on that piece of paper.

"Coach, you got a minute?"

It was Learie's dad Greg and he didn't look happy.

"Not really," said Coach Dunn. "Can we set up a time to talk tomorrow afternoon? Let me know what time is good and I can give you a call."

"No, we need to talk now! You're not treating my son very well. You've shown me time and again that you don't care about him and you refuse to give him opportunities even though he is a captain. That actually makes things worse. How can you sit your captain?"

"I appreciate your concern for Learie. I know that he appreciates your support of him and his teammates by attending all of these games, but this isn't the time nor place to talk about this. I'd be glad to …"

Coach Dunn wasn't able to finish as Learie's dad interrupted him.

"No, this is exactly the time and place. He doesn't need to get lost any deeper in your doghouse. You need to understand how your coaching is affecting him."

It was obvious to Coach Dunn that Learie's dad was getting more and more heated, and he needed to try to defuse the situation.

"We don't have practice tomorrow at all, so that'd be a great time to talk. We'll both probably be less emotional, and we can talk through some things. Let me ask you, what's the thing that you are most frustrated with right now and we'll be sure to address that tomorrow?"

"That's easy. You called for him to go into the game and then pulled him back and made him go sit back down. That was embarrassing!"

"For you or Learie?" asked Coach Dunn.

"It doesn't matter. You just don't treat people that way."

"Well, I'll be glad to talk with you tomorrow about your perception of how I treat Learie. We'll also need to discuss his questionable attitude and lack of responsibility, despite being a captain as you point out. But specifically, in regard to tonight, right before Learie went to the scorer's table, he asked me who I wanted him to guard on defense. I asked him what he meant and Learie said, 'do you want me to guard the man guarding me or someone else'?"

"That's a great question Coach! What's wrong with that? Don't you want your players asking good questions? Don't you want them knowing who they're guarding? Don't you want them to ask questions when they're confused?"

"Yes, I absolutely want them asking good questions but a question that they should already know the answer to is not a GOOD question."

"It seems to me that you were too hard on him. How is Learie supposed to know whether you think a question is a good one or bad one?"

"In the timeout less than two minutes before that, I told the entire team that we were going to play our Blitz Matchup Zone for the rest of the game no matter the situation. Learie was not paying attention at all. I'm pretty sure that he was checking out the crowd or something like that but Learie was definitely not ready to go into the game. I wasn't going to reward him for not being responsible, especially as a captain."

Just then, Mr. Frank approached the two men.

"Sorry to interrupt fellas, but Coach, the trainer needs to talk with you about Jaylen's leg. I'm sorry about that. I'm sure you fellas can probably catch up tomorrow or the next day."

"Thanks, Mr. Frank," said Coach Dunn

As he turned to head toward the training room, Coach Dunn said, "Greg, please text me and let me know when you want to talk tomorrow."

Once Coach Dunn had walked away, Mr. Frank turned his attention to Learie's dad.

"Hey, Greg. Good to see you. I hope that I didn't interrupt anything too pressing."

"Well, I have been frustrated all year and it kind of came to a head tonight. It's actually probably good that you came when you did," said Learie's dad.

"Why's that, Greg," Mr. Frank asked him.

"I think I might have jumped to conclusions a little too quickly or at least been wrong on one thing. I'm not super happy, but I need some time to think about what Coach said."

"Well, glad to hear it. I know we've been friends for a while, and I know you love Learie, but I also know that you want the team to be successful. Part of that is at least giving the coach a chance to explain things and discuss things with you. I hope you fellas are able to work it out tomorrow. Like I said, good to see you and have a good trip home."

"You too, Frank. Don't drink too many of those energy drinks. You'll have to make way too many pit stops," Greg said with a wink.

TRAINING ROOM

Although Coach Dunn was glad to be leaving the situation with Learie's dad, he dreaded what awaited him as he headed toward the athletic training room.

"How's Jaylen?" Coach Dunn asked Angela.

Angela had been the Eagles' trainer for many years. She was very good at what she did. Angela was knowledgeable and extremely caring. She had a great mix of personality and wisdom. She could put players and coaches at ease but also knew where the boundaries were. She was a true professional and the Eagles were lucky to have her.

"It's not good," Angela replied. "We won't know for certain until tomorrow when we can get an MRI, but I'm guessing that it's completely torn, and he'll miss the remainder of the season."

This was not the news Coach was hoping for. The season had been challenging enough with Jaylen running the point guard position and doing all he could to help the team. He was someone that always did what coach asked and he did it with a smile. He wasn't the most gifted, but he was smart, tough, and had a positive attitude. It seemed like everyone liked Jaylen. It still amazed him that Jaylen and Learie were roommates. They seemed to be polar opposites with their attitudes and sense of responsibility.

"I'm really sorry about this Jaylen. Hang in there, buddy," said Coach Dunn.

"I just can't believe my season might be over. This hasn't been a good year, but I was determined to do all I could to help us on the court to finish strong," said Jaylen.

"I know that. Let's wait and see what the doctor says tomorrow," said Coach Dunn. "But, if it's torn and you're out for the rest of the season, you can still help us turn this season around. We only have about six weeks left but there are enough games for us to finish strong. You might not be able to lead from the court, but you can certainly lead from the bench."

"Thanks, coach. I will do what I can."

"I know you will. You control the controllable, Jaylen, and you definitely know how to bring the energy and positivity to the team. You can do that wherever you're at, whether it be the court or the bench."

Angela brought over some crutches and handed them to Jaylen.

"I think Jaylen can serve as a good role model for the team," she said. "And you're right he'll provide enthusiasm and energy even though he isn't playing. I think he can be infectious, but in a good way."

Coach Dunn shook his head in agreement and patted Jaylen on the back, "I'll see you on the bus."

After Coach Dunn had left the training room to go to the media center, Angela, Jaylen, and Travis were the only Eagles remaining in the training room.

"I can't believe that you got hurt," Travis said from another training table. "You bring so much energy to the team. You've got to be the hardest worker I've ever been around. Your effort is incredible. Day in and day out, it doesn't matter."

"I appreciate that, Travis. But I don't do anything special. I've just always played hard because I knew that one day my basketball career would be over, and I didn't want to look back and have any regrets. Looks like my season might be over a little sooner than expected but I still have no regrets other than I wasn't able to help us get more wins."

"You did what you could," said Travis. "But maybe the season isn't over. Maybe you'll just be out for like a week or something."

"Hope so but the reality is that Angela is pretty good at what she does, and she has prepared me for the possibility that I'm done. She thinks that even if it isn't officially torn all the way, that it might be difficult to come back from this in the month or so we have left in the season. I'm starting to prepare myself mentally that this is probably it for me."

Jaylen was tough and had a good attitude, but it was obvious that the thought of missing the remainder of the season was hard on him. He was trying to stay optimistic around Travis. He knew that Travis looked up to him ever since Jaylen hosted Travis on a recruiting visit last year. Travis came from a good background. He was a solid player and a good student. Jaylen could see a little bit of himself in Travis as he didn't excel at anything but also didn't have many obvious flaws.

"You're the energy for our team. I'm not sure what we'll do without you. It certainly won't be the same," said Travis.

"But it can be. What I bring to the team is probably the easiest skill a person can have. Giving consistent effort and providing energy is something that anyone can do regardless of size, athletic ability, status on the team, or shooting ability," Jaylen pointed out.

"You say that but if it's so easy, why don't more players bust their tail like you do?" Travis asked.

"That's a great question," said Jaylen. "Unfortunately, I was never very big or fast. I also was not as naturally gifted shooting the ball like James or Antonio. I had to find other ways to make myself valuable. Certainly, I knew a positive attitude could help but I had to do more. I had to go further than that. I had to find a way to turn that positive attitude into a basketball skill. I figured that I could outwork other people."

Jaylen adjusted the ice pack on his knee before continuing his answer.

"I figured I could hustle on the court. I could be aggressive. If I got into shape and stayed in shape, then I'd be able to do these things much longer than someone else. When other players got tired, I'd be the one getting rebounds, deflections, steals, and outrunning people down the court. I might not be good enough to score on people in the half-court, but if they were tired or loafing then I could gain an edge. It's worked well for me through the years."

"I wish that I could do what you do."

Jaylen responded to Travis, "That's the thing. What I do shouldn't be special. Anyone can do it. You definitely can do it. It's a mentality. It's me saying every day that I will be the last one to quit. It's me saying that I will get every loose ball. It's me saying that I'm going to fire up our team through my play on the court."

Though Travis hadn't really thought of all this in the way Jaylen was explaining it, Travis was locked in on what he was saying. It sounded so simple as he listened to Jaylen break it down.

"I always think in terms of what can I do today that will bring us momentum?" continued Jaylen. "You can do that very thing also. It's baby steps. You build habits practice after practice and play after play. It starts with just deciding that you want to be a person that puts forth effort and brings energy."

"But I don't really play much," Travis stated.

"How we perform in games is usually a direct reflection of how we've prepared," Jaylen responded. "You build habits daily, not in just a day. You can decide today that you will be this way but then each day, you have to recommit to that mentality and go out and do it. Touching the lines on sprints instead of turning six inches too soon, not standing up on defense, sprinting the floor every time regardless if you'll get the ball, or blocking out on every shot are just some of the ways you can become this kind of player. It starts in practice and will eventually become automatic for you."

"I definitely could improve in those areas."

"We all can do better," admitted Jaylen. "It's easy to be a spectator and watch shots go up without hitting the boards. But when we have a mentality that every shot is a miss, then it's easier to rebound. Some players struggle when they aren't getting shots, or they're playing with a ball hog. Playing with a ball hog can actually be good."

That last statement threw Travis for a loop and confused him.

"Wait, what? How's that possible? I've got to hear this one."

"Well, think about it," Jaylen said. "If a ball hog shoots the ball, then two things could happen. First, the ball goes in the basket, which is a good thing for our team. Our team scored and that's what we should be wanting on every possession. The second thing that can happen is the ball hog misses the shot. If this happens just think of their shot as a pass to you. It just happened to hit the rim or the backboard first. If you have a ball hog that misses five, six, seven, or even more shots in a game then that's a lot of opportunities for you to go get an extra basket. That's also probably more opportunities than the number of plays Coach will call for you during the course of the game. It's really just a mindset. Hustle is a talent and I'm going find every way possible to cash in on that talent."

"I never really thought of that stuff," said Travis.

"Even the best shooter will be off some nights. There will be some days when the ball just doesn't bounce our way. But my hustle and effort will never have an off night. I determine my effort. Not the coach, not the officials, not my teammates, and not the circumstances. I'm the only one that can control how hard I work," Jaylen pointed out.

"Even though I'm a freshman riding the bench, I think that I can start applying some of this stuff you said. I'm going to try it," said Travis.

"When I was a freshman, I experienced some of the same things that you may be struggling with," said Jaylen. "It was a big jump up in level of play and some of the things I did in high school didn't work as easily at this level. I wasn't playing as much as maybe I expected coming out of high school. Let me tell you what Coach did my freshman year that I'll never forget."

SPARK PLUG

Angela came over and replaced Jaylen's ice pack with an elastic wrap and a knee brace that would secure his knee temporarily until they got back to their home training room. Jaylen thanked her and then continued telling Travis about his freshman year.

"Anyway, Coach knew that my dad was into cars and so he took a shot that I knew something about cars, as well. He asked me what my dream car was. I told him that it was a Lamborghini. He told me something that I'll never forget. He told me that a little sparkplug costing five to ten dollars could keep that rich-man's car from running. On the flip side, that little inexpensive spark plug can deliver electric current from the ignition system to the combustion chamber."

"The what to the why?" Travis asked, obviously confused. "You kind of lost me there at the end. Sorry, I'm not much of a car guy."

"Sorry about that," apologized Jaylen. "A spark plug is just something that provides a spark. It ignites an engine. It provides energy. An expensive car can't run without it. Our team might be talented but if not for energy. If not for spark plugs, then the individual talents on a team are wasted. Without a spark plug, a Lamborghini sits useless in the garage. Every car needs spark plugs. Every team needs them, also."

"So, you're the spark plug on this team?" asked Travis.

"Well, I'm one of them," Jaylen replied. "The best teams have 12 spark plugs. The best teams have everyone giving energy and effort. I do what I can. I hope that my play inspires others and motivates others to play harder, but I can't make you or anyone else want it. You've got to decide for yourself. I do hope, though, that my style of play and effort can be infectious, in a good way, like Angela said earlier."

Angela was in the corner packing up some equipment but was still listening to the conversation. She smiled when she heard him mention what she'd said earlier. It always made her feel good when the players listened to what she said. She cared about the student-athletes. Not only did she want them to be physically strong and healthy, but she wanted them to develop as people.

Jaylen continued, "We're either energy givers or takers. We can be a vampire and suck the life out of the team or be an oxygen mask, breathing life into the team. We can complain or go through the motions. We can do the bare minimum, or we can make others better. We can be positive. We can try to generate momentum even when things might seem at a standstill. No matter our talent, we can always provide energy."

"I've seen the success you've had with working so hard," said Travis. "It's got to be worth it."

"Just look at some of the best players in the world," said Jaylen. "They aren't lazy. They don't take many plays off. There are plenty of talented players that don't fulfill their potential. Everyone in college is talented. Everyone in the NBA is talented. What separates the best? What takes certain players from good to great? Talent is never enough. Being a better shooter or dribbler or being able to jump over people doesn't make a player good. It just makes them talented at those things. If you combine those talents with effort and energy, now you've got the potential for a great player."

Angela finished putting the last piece of equipment into the sports medicine travel bag and then walked over to the two players.

"I have the luxury of watching everything from a distance and observing," noted Angela. "Jaylen certainly works hard. His energy can be contagious. There are some other players that will do this on occasion, but they aren't consistent. Jaylen brings it every day, not just when he's feeling good. In fact, there have been a few times that he's been sick or not feeling good and you wouldn't have known it. Travis, if you really want to have this mentality Jaylen talks about then you can do it. It's your choice. It might not get you more playing time right away, but it'll another step closer to getting this team where it needs to be."

"What do you mean?" asked Travis.

"Have you ever been to a huge professional sporting event where they do the wave?" asked Angela.

Travis shook his head up and down. He'd been to a lot of Saturday afternoon tailgates and college football games growing up with his dad and brothers.

Angela continued with her thought, "I bet you've never seen an announcement on the big jumbotron asking you to do the wave. You've probably never heard the announcer tell you that it was time for the wave."

"Now that you mention it, I haven't. How do those things start?" Travis asked.

"Great question. That's my point," said Angela. "It starts with one or two people getting one or two people to do it with them. Then another couple of people start to do it and then more. Eventually, you have a whole section and then another and then another and then the whole stadium is doing the wave."

"All because one drunk yahoo started the wave?" asked Travis.

"Right, except they don't necessarily have to be drunk or a yahoo, for that matter," replied Angela. "If you want to influence your team. If you want to be a valuable part of this team whether you're playing or not. Then, be that person that starts the wave. Be that person that ignites and energizes your team. Be the change that you want to see on this team."

Jaylen said, "Be a yahoo, Travis! Start the wave on our team."

"There's that but in listening to you talk, not just today, but at other times, I believe that you want more for this team," continued Angela. "If that's the case, then let that change start with you. It might be more important than ever now that Jaylen is hurt. Somebody has to pick up the baton and run with it. Somebody has to be the guy that takes over as the spark plug on the court. If not in games, at least in practice, where you can build positive habits. Who knows, maybe you will get the other yahoos in the other sections of the stadium to follow your lead."

"I think I can be the yahoo this team needs," Travis said with a smile.

"Awesome," said Jaylen. "I guess I have a new partner in crime when it comes to trying to infect our teammates with enthusiasm, energy and a desire to work hard."

"I'm in. Thanks for talking to me Jaylen," said Travis. "Also, thank you, Angela, for inspiring me to be a yahoo."

"You're welcome," said Angela. "Now, you two better get out of here and on that bus. You don't want James and Antonio to get on first."

LEAVING THE GYM

When Coach Dunn got on the bus, it was noisy. Players were interacting loudly, music was being played that should have been quieted by headphones, and there were plenty of cell phone conversations that should have stayed private.

It was bad enough they just lost a game in an embarrassing fashion, but he was unfairly confronted by a parent. To top it all off, Jaylen was most likely out for the season. Now, he had to put up with noise on the bus.

It wasn't even an hour since his locker room tirade. He had no choice but to wonder if they even cared at all.

"Quiet down back there!" demanded Coach. "At least, act like you care that we lost tonight."

"We care," responded Bobbi.

This was the attitude he'd want to see from Bobbi. Even though he was a freshman, he was a starter and seemed to have the right mentality. Coach Dunn had high hopes for Bobbi and thought he had a bright future if he didn't get contaminated by some of the poor habits some of the team's "leaders" demonstrated.

"You might care, but it's obvious that most of your teammates don't care," Coach Dunn said to Bobbi.

He then turned his attention to everybody again.

"You guys think you care but if you truly did then you'd act like it. We just lost a game we shouldn't have lost and nobody would know it by how you're behaving right now. Most people might even think you won. You don't care. You're not focused. You're not committed. I'm not even saying that just because of how you're acting right now on the bus. It's more than that."

Coach Dunn was getting more and more frustrated. He had not been able to figure out this team as he had done with past teams. Everything was starting to come to a head, and he had to get a few more things off his chest that he hadn't said in his short post-game locker room talk.

"If you actually cared, you'd stand up for people when they come to the bench after leaving the game. You'd help teammates up off the ground. You'd practice hard so that you could play hard. You'd act like champions instead of just participants. Sometimes I think this is just glorified intramurals or you're just playing pickup. No commitment. No investment."

The stat sheet Coach Dunn was looking at after the game told him about outcomes but the reasons behind many of those numbers and results were often because of these very things he was now talking about.

Coach Dunn continued, "You guys say you care but you just glance over scouting reports. You don't get enough sleep at night. You criticize one another. You criticize coaches. You don't rebound for each other during shootaround. Everyone wants their own shots. You don't touch the lines during sprints. You don't block out on every shot. You don't dive for loose balls. No, you don't care as much as you should. "

Even though he had everyone's attention now, he decided to use a slightly different approach as he continued.

"You remember those ham and egg breakfast sandwiches we got you this morning. Those eggs came from a hen somewhere that was involved in the process. That hen participated in your breakfast. But that ham, oh that ham. That ham came from a pig who was 100% committed to your breakfast. That pig was completely invested in your breakfast. Are you like the hen or the pig when it comes to this team? You say you care. You say you are committed but are you 100% all-in or just merely participating and going through the motions? Some of you participate in basketball. You're involved in this sport, but you're not committed like the pig was committed to your breakfast. You'll say that you're committed but people will know when you are committed. You don't have to tell them."

Coach Dunn was on a roll now and he was just getting started on his soapbox.

"Have any of you ever heard of the Spanish explorer Cortez?" he asked.

The players shook their heads but even if somebody knew, they wouldn't dare interrupt Coach Dunn at this point.

"Way back in the day, Cortez and his men landed in Mexico and was attempting to colonize that land for Spain, but they were going to face the mighty Aztec Indians. He sensed that his men were a little bit fearful. To motivate them, Cortez ordered that all the boats be burned. There was no turning around. No turning back. Retreat was not an option. They were all-in. They had each other's backs because there wasn't an alternative. That's a real commitment."

Coach Dunn might have been finished with the Cortez story, but he wasn't done trying to make his point. There was still enough time left in the season for a turnaround. He didn't know if this particular team could change their mentality, but he was determined to keep trying to inspire them.

Coach Dunn continued, "How many of you have ever thrown up because you went so hard? I'm not talking throwing up because you ate something before working out, or because you were hungover, or because you were out of shape. I'm talking because you went so hard. You pushed yourself to the limit. You went beyond what you thought you were capable of. Very few people work hard enough to feel that.

Most people don't outwork their talent. The best players in the world are the best, not because they are talented, but because they maximize their talent by outworking their talent. Whether you can jump out of the gym, run faster than anyone, or you're lacking in physical talents, you can always work harder than your baseline talent. By outworking your talent, average players can become good and good players can become great."

Coach Dunn didn't want to stay too long on this soapbox but as long as he had some of their attention, he needed to take advantage of this moment.

"What about you guys?" Coach Dunn asked the team as they all sat in their seats. "So far this year, all you've done is the bare minimum. You're just getting by. Some of you probably can't wait for the season to end. How do you think that attitude affects your play? You can't have a negative mindset and, at the same time, be positive in your lives. Do you know what the best do better than everyone else? They come early, stay late, and do a little bit extra. They keep fighting when they're down. They refuse to quit, even if things don't go their way. They don't see obstacles, distractions, or impossibilities because they're too focused on their goals. What they want most is much more important than what is easiest right now. They know their priorities and are committed to them!"

What was once a noisy bus just minutes earlier was now eerily quiet. The players sat silently in their seats. Some of them digesting what Coach Dunn had just said, while still a few just waited anxiously for him to finish so they could go back to their own cares and concerns.

"Coach, can I say something?" asked Mr. Frank.

MR. FRANK

Coach Dunn had just said a lot of good things, but it seemed that Mr. Frank had something to share and Coach Dunn never missed an opportunity to let Mr. Frank speak and share some insights. He often asked Mr. Frank to say a few words. He and Mr. Frank had developed quite a feel for one another through the years. Mr. Frank always seemed to have perfect timing as he shared just the right insight.

Coach Dunn trusted Mr. Frank implicitly. Before becoming a bus driver, Mr. Frank had been a policeman, firefighter, and even a truck driver with over a million miles driven without so much as a speeding ticket or a fender bender. He had even served humbly in local politics for many years. Even though he was getting up there in years, Mr. Frank still volunteered with little league baseball and was involved in many civic organizations. His life had been all about making good decisions and helping others. Mr. Frank was full of wisdom and Coach Dunn never questioned his intentions or agenda.

"Sure, Mr. Frank. I'm betting that half of these guys have already stopped listening to what I was saying, anyway. Maybe they'll listen to you."

"Oh, I don't know about that, Coach. I think these fellas know that you're only saying what you're saying because you care about them.

You want them to be their best. But as you were talking, I thought of a story I heard years ago that really stuck with me and it might stick with them also."

Coach Dunn sat down, nodding at Mr. Frank to continue.

"Fellas, I know that the season hasn't gone quite like you wanted it to go. Some of you might be frustrated with each other, with Coach, or with any number of people or things. I understand being frustrated. But, have any of you ever heard of R.U. Darby?"

Mr. Frank could see a collective shaking of the head back and forth by the 12 Eagles.

"I didn't think so. R.U. Darby was one of the original San Francisco 49ers. Now, I'm not talking Joe Montana, Jerry Rice, or Jimmy G's 49ers but the 1800's prospecting for gold type 49ers. You see, R.U. Darby was from the East Coast but relocated to California during the gold rush of 1849. Day after day, he searched for unfathomable riches. He had all the best equipment but couldn't seem to find that mother lode. Sure, he found some nuggets here and there, but it wasn't what he wanted. Finally, he got frustrated because things weren't going the way he wanted. Do you fellas know what he did when he got frustrated and thought he was just wasting his time?

"I'm guessing that something probably went his way," said Bobbi. "Since you're telling us this story, I'm guessing that he overcame those frustrations. He probably caught a break, found gold, and stopped being frustrated, right Mr. Frank?"

"Good guess, Bobbi, but actually just the opposite happened. When R.U. Darby got frustrated, he quit. He sold his equipment and the rights to the land he was working on to somebody else. Those people immediately went to work on his land and with his equipment. They ended up finding the mother lode of gold just three feet from where R.U. Darby had stopped. He was just three feet away from the goal – and the gold – he had been working toward. He quit too soon. He gave in to his frustrations and quit three feet from riches untold."

Mr. Frank paused letting the story hang out there for a moment until James broke the silence with a comment that was probably on most of the player's minds.

"Seriously, I wouldn't be able to live with myself if that happened to me. That dude sure messed up."

"You're right, James," Mr. Frank responded. "R.U. Darby sure did mess up. But I remember that story every time I start to get frustrated with how things are going in my life. Every time that I think about quitting or pouting or just getting plain complacent about things, I'm reminded about R.U. Darby. The same applies to basketball. You never know when everything is going to click. You never know when you are going to get your opportunity in practice or a game. You never know when the breaks will start coming your way. But if you quit. If you lose focus. If you allow frustration to overwhelm you, then you'll never be prepared or ready to cash in if and when your reward comes."

"Preach it, Mr. Frank! Say it a little louder for the people in the back," said Brandon.

Raising his voice, Mr. Frank said, "IF YOU QUIT. IF YOU LOSE FOCUS. IF YOU…"

"Mr. Frank. Mr. Frank, I was just messing with you," said Brandon with a slight chuckle. "It's an expression. It's a way of saying you just dropped some truth bombs. I think everyone heard you the first time."

"Oh, okay. I have a hard time keeping up with all these things that you fellas say. Regardless, enough with the talking. We need to get on the road so we can get some food in your bellies."

Coach Dunn always appreciated the insights Mr. Frank provided throughout the years. Mr. Frank always seemed to know just the right thing to say and when to say it. This story about R.U. Darby was no exception. Coach Dunn believed that Mr. Frank had just hit another home run with this story and that it might stick with a couple of the players.

"Sounds good, Mr. Frank. Thanks for sharing."

Turning to the Eagles, Coach Dunn said, "Let's think about the story Mr. Frank just told us and how it relates to our commitment to our goals and commitment to each other. Also, and guys, please keep the noise to a minimum."

Mr. Frank checked his mirrors and slowly edge out of the parking lot onto the road. The day had been a tough one already and they still had quite a haul in front of them.

TRAFFIC JAM

It was only supposed to take 15 minutes to get from the gym to the restaurant but as the Eagles had learned all too often this season, sometimes things just don't go as planned.

"We just left the gym and we're already stuck in traffic. How is that even possible?" questioned Drew.

"I know Mr. Frank is like an All-Conference bus driver but I agree. It's weird that we're stopped already. I hope we get moving soon," James added.

The team had been consumed with other things and hadn't noticed the first few minutes of the traffic jam. Now, however, they were going on ten minutes of not moving an inch on this two-lane road. To a bunch of hungry and frustrated players, ten minutes seemed like an eternity.

"Why did we go this way?" Drew continued to complain. "There had to have been a better route, right?"

"Hey Mr. Frank, don't you have some kind of traffic app on your phone?" James asked.

"Sorry fellas. This was the best route to take but we've got a broken-down car or something like that not too far in front of us. We're not on the freeway yet so there really isn't any room for us to go around. And we can't back this thing up with all the traffic behind us. I'm afraid we're just going to have to wait it out. Hopefully, it won't be much longer. Fortunately, from what I can tell, it's not a major fender-bender or anything like that. Please be patient, fellas.

"Yeah, patience is a virtue, right?" said Drew with a hint of sarcasm.

"Yes, it is," Mr. Frank replied. "But remember that patience isn't just about our ability to wait. It's also about our attitude while we wait."

"And with that, we just got hit with another truth bomb from Mr. Frank," said James.

"That's nice but it doesn't put food in my stomach. I'm still starving," said Drew.

"If you're that hungry, go grab something from the snack box," suggested the co-captain Brandon.

"I need real food. I nearly played a whole game today. I need more than just fruit or some crackers. I'm seriously starting to get hangry!" Drew said emphatically.

"I agree that a spicy chicken sandwich is better than a banana but that's all we have right now. Guess, you have a choice to make," Brandon responded.

"Seriously, how does this stuff always happen to me," moaned Drew.

"Hey Drew, cut it out," Brandon snapped back. "You aren't the only one that's hungry. We all are. Think of something else. Stop talking about food, it's not helping. Mr. Frank is doing all that he can do right now. Sometimes things are going to happen that are outside our control. Let it go."

"We could have gone a different way!" said Drew.

Jaylen had been listening to Drew and thought of something that might help Drew see a different perspective on their current circumstances.

"You're right, Drew," Jaylen said. "But we don't know that something wouldn't have happened going that way either. Just make the best of it. Remember that sign in our locker room that says, 'Life is 10% what happens to you and 90% how you react to what happens to you'. Well, the traffic is the 10% and you complaining is the 90%."

"Hey Drew, do you remember last year on that trip when the TV screens weren't working, and they just stayed blue the whole time?" asked Brandon.

"Yes, that was funny – not funny cause we couldn't watch TV – but still, funny," Said Drew as you remembered that bus ride.

"We made everything into a blue joke for the next couple of weeks," said Brandon. "Coach, are we having bluuuuueberriers for breakfast? Coach, when do we get the scouting report for our Bluuuuuefield game? Coach, when we go to Vegas for that tournament, can we watch the Bluuuuueman group?" said Brandon enjoying the funny memories.

"Yeah, that was probably pretty annoying for Coach come to think about it, but I certainly got a kick out of it," said Jaylen.

Brandon recalled, "We laugh about it now and we even laughed about it then because we weren't focused on the 10%. You know, the TV not working."

"Instead, we focused on the jokes we could make up," said Drew.

"You're right," said Brandon. "And that was the 90% that the locker room sign talks about."

Just then, Jaylen interrupted them, "Hey, you feel that? I think we're moving again."

Indeed, the bus had started to ease forward ever so slightly but it was progress, nonetheless. Slowly but surely, the bus approached a broken-down car on the road. It must have run over some nails or something because it had not one, but two flat tires.

Fortunately, the driver was able to control it enough not to crash but he wasn't able to get it off to the side of the road.

"Look, that car has a couple of flat tires," observed Brandon.

"I'm glad that we don't have flat tires," said Drew. "We'd have waited in traffic even longer and I'd be even hungrier. Maybe now we can go get a chicken sandwich."

"I can taste it now. I can't wait to get some chicken. But you know what Drew?" Brandon asked.

"What?" said Drew.

"I'm thinking that your attitude back there was similar to that car," said Brandon.

"What do you mean by that?" asked Drew.

"Well, that car couldn't go anywhere with flat tires and you weren't getting anywhere with your bad attitude. Your attitude was like a flat tire. You can't go very far until you change it," said Brandon with a smile.

"Ha Ha. Very funny. When's your Netflix comedy special, by the way?" Drew snapped back with a smile of his own.

"I thought it was kind of witty, but I was really going for something similar to what Mr. Frank might say."

"It was close. Good try," said Drew.

TIME TO EAT

Mr. Frank pulled the bus into the restaurant's parking lot.

"Finally! I'm starving," said Drew to anyone who would listen.

"Make sure that your travel suits are on as we go in," Coach Dunn reminded the team. "Remember that you're representing the Eagles. Also, stick to your $10 meal limit."

Once all of the players and coaches had piled off the bus, Mr. Frank drove it around back, out of the way of the other customers.

Coach Dunn thought that it was always interesting to see who rushed to the front of the line. They would all get their food quickly. In fact, they often came to this restaurant and it never ceased to amaze him how quickly they prepared the food orders.

"I will take a #1 with no pickles but with extra tomatoes," said Learie.

"What drink would you like with your combo?" asked the lady at the register.

"Sweet Tea."

"You got it."

"Thank you."

"My pleasure," she said. "I'll gladly serve the next guest."

A similar conversation repeated itself over and over again until all of the players and coaches had their trays of food and had found their seats. Actually, there was one player who didn't have his food, or at least the correct food that he ordered. Drew approached the lady at the register.

"Hey, this isn't right," announced Drew. "You got my order wrong"

"What seems to be the problem?" she asked.

"I ordered a spicy chicken sandwich, and this isn't a spicy sandwich at all," Drew complained.

"I'm sorry about that. Did you order the deluxe or just the regular?"

"I ordered the deluxe but that doesn't even matter right now because what you gave me isn't even spicy. Never mind all the pickles, tomatoes, lettuce, and whatever else makes it deluxe."

"I understand. I'm sorry for your inconvenience. Let me retake your order and we'll get it out to you as soon as we can," she said.

"Okay," said Drew shaking his head as he walked away from the counter.

Just a few minutes later, tray in hand, the lady from the register walked Drew's food over to him.

"Sorry about the delay, and the mess up," she said. "Here's a coupon for a complimentary ice cream cone as a small token from us to you. We regret that your dining experience wasn't what you expected."

"Yeah, thanks. I'm sure you guys didn't do it on purpose," Drew replied. "Finally, I'm starving! I absolutely love these spicy deluxe sandwiches!"

It tasted as good as it always did.

Just then, Demetrius sat down at the table next to them and began talking loud enough for everyone to hear.

"You should have heard Bobbi just now in the bathroom. He was complaining that he's never had a worse sandwich here than what he ate tonight. It was kind of funny. He wasn't throwing up or anything.

That would have stunk if he'd had a reaction. You all know that he is a mental midget when it comes to hot sauce. He's a ketchup guy, you know. Anyway, he was complaining that his sandwich didn't taste right. He was like 'you guys played a prank on me and emptied one of those hot sauce packets on my sandwich when I wasn't looking. I was sweating bullets eating that thing'. It was so funny. I don't know what he was talking about but it sure was funny."

Drew interrupted, "Wait. Bobbi said it was too hot?"

"Oh yeah, you know how soft he is. Always cheese or veggie pizza because the pepperoni is too spicy," chuckled Demetrius.

When Bobbi came out of the bathroom, all eyes were on him.

"What?" Bobbi asked confused.

"Caliente," Demetrius joked.

"Oh, okay. I get it" as Bobbi gave his roommate the evil eye.

"Hey, Bobbi. Your sandwich was too spicy?" asked Drew.

"Alright, I get it. You guys are having your fun with me," said Bobbi.

"No, seriously. I'm asking for real. Was your sandwich actually spicy?" Drew asked again.

"My mouth was dying but I fought through it like a champ," said Bobbi. "I wasn't going to quit or give up like that gold dude Mr. Frank was talking about earlier tonight."

"I don't think he had your taste buds and bad food in mind when he was saying not to give up," joked Demetrius.

"Seriously though, back to your sandwich," said Drew. "I got an absolutely plain sandwich and I raised a stink at the counter. I blamed them. What was your order number?"

"Let me check," said Bobbi as he looked through the crumpled-up napkins and straw wrappers on his table. "Here it is. Number nine."

"Bobbi, that's a six," said Demetrius looking over Bobbi's shoulder. "Seriously, and you're the one with a4.0-grade point average?"

"My order number was a nine," said Drew. "You took my food. Serves you right. No wonder it tasted spicy. It was exactly that – a spicy sandwich. Just like Demetrius said, how are you a 4.0?"

"Man, I don't know. Let's just forget about it," Bobbi requested.

"Except, that I gave the lady up at the counter a hard time. I thought that they messed up the order but all along, we were the ones that had messed things up."

"Oops," said Bobbi.

"Oops is right. I kind of feel bad," said Drew.

James was never shy about inserting himself into a conversation, so he decided this was as good of a time as any.

"You could always apologize. I've been told that is what I should do when I make my girl mad."

"Oh, you've been told, have you?" Antonio asked his roommate. "I'm not sure you've ever listened to that advice. Plus, if you had, you'd probably always be apologizing for something."

Walking past Antonio and James as they bantered back and forth, Drew approached the lady from the register as she was putting away the broom and closing the storage closet door.

"Yes, sir. How may I help you?" she asked.

"Uhmm. Yeah, ah. I think I messed up with the spicy chicken sandwich. Sorry about that" apologized Drew

"What do you mean?" she asked.

"One of my teammates had it all along. I just assumed that you must have screwed up. I didn't even think that it'd be my fault. Sorry about that," Drew said.

"I understand," she said. "I'm just glad that we were able to get you a replacement sandwich quickly enough. Does your friend need the sandwich that he ordered or is he okay?"

"Nah, he's good. Though it was a bit too hot for him."

"Okay, well we just want to make sure that you have a good experience here. We take pride in our food and our service."

"I guess the customer isn't always right," Drew said.

"None of us are right all the time. We realize that but that doesn't stop us from still trying to serve you and find a solution to the problem if we're able to," she said.

"When you waited on me the second time, did you know that I was the one that had made the mistake?" Drew asked.

"We don't worry about who's to blame," she said. "Life can be pretty miserable if we're always pointing fingers or playing the blame game. Instead of determining who is to blame, we try to take responsibility for things. It might not have been our fault, but we can be responsible for doing what we can to make a situation better. In your case, it was easy to make another sandwich."

"Thanks for that and sorry once again," Drew said as he turned to walk away.

"It's our pleasure to serve you," she said.

Drew turned back toward the lady as she said that.

"Can I ask you a question?" he asked.

"Sure, what is it?" she wondered.

"You keep saying words like 'serve' and 'our pleasure'. I don't hear people at other restaurants talk like that. Why do you guys say that stuff?" asked Drew.

"Good question. Obviously, we think we have the best chicken around but more importantly, we feel like our job is to serve. Whether we're a new employee, a cook, someone who sweeps the floors, the manager, or the owner – no matter our role or title, we want to treat our customers like friends. We want to be kind to everyone."

The lady continued to explain to Drew what made the restaurant different than all the others.

"You see, every life has a story. Every customer is a person. We want to go the extra mile and make someone's life a little better today. If I had worried about who was right and who was wrong about your chicken sandwich, then I wouldn't have been trying to make your day better. I would just have tried to get my way or be right. In general, we've found that the best leaders are those who serve. People tend to follow them with their hearts and buy into what they are selling."

Drew was still listening to the lady and she could tell that he was interested in what she was saying.

"It might be weird or different, but I hope that it makes sense," she continued. "I might have gone a little deep on you, but I get excited talking about this stuff. I don't just work here because I want to collect a paycheck. There are plenty of jobs out there for that. I truly enjoy the people I work with but also the people – the friends, if you will – that I get to interact with every day, like you and your teammates."

"That's cool. Thanks for sharing all of that. I never really thought of any of that stuff before." Drew said.

"By the way, what kind of ice cream cone do you want with that coupon I gave you earlier?" she asked Drew.

"Seriously? Even though you know that I was the one that screwed up?" Drew said with some confusion. "Here, you can have that coupon back. Use it for someone that deserves it."

"It's not about deserving or not. We gave that to you, and we expect you to use it. You're not going to refuse us the joy of being kind to you, are you?" She asked with a sly smile.

"So, will that be chocolate or vanilla?"

Drew smiled.

12

LEAVING THE RESTAURANT

As the players left the restaurant most of them showed some appreciation or at least acknowledged Coach with a quick head nod as he held the door open for all of them.

"Thanks," said Drew.

"You're welcome," said Coach.

"Don't you mean, 'My Pleasure'? joked Drew.

"Well-played," Coach Dunn said. "Now get on the bus. You were just about the last one."

"Lucky for me James and Antonio are still my teammates. With them around, I'll never have to worry about being last," said Drew as he boarded the bus.

Coach smiled as James and Antonio finally sauntered past him, and as usual, were the last players to board the bus.

"Hey coach, now that you finally decided to join us, everybody's on the bus. Time to make moves," said James as Coach got on the bus.

"Very funny," Coach snapped back.

Antonio fist-bumped James and said, "We're just messing with you, Coach. We saw you practicing for your next date with your wife by holding the door open for everybody. But seriously, why were you doing that?"

"It's just the right thing to do," Coach Dunn replied. "I don't always do what's right, unfortunately, but I still try to be a servant leader whenever I can."

"Servant leader? What's that mean?" asked Antonio.

"It really just means that I'm leading by serving others," said Coach Dunn.

"That sounds like one of those oxymorons. How can you lead and serve at the same time?" James asked.

"Serving others just means that I'm trying to help others. It means that I'm trying to take care of you and your needs. Holding the door isn't a big deal but it's something I could do to be nice," Coach Dunn pointed out.

Drew was listening to the conversation and spoke up, "Hey Coach, it's funny you should say that. Do you remember when they didn't give me the right sandwich?"

"Yes, you seemed a little frustrated by the whole thing. But they apologized and seemed to have patience even though you were a little short with them," said Coach Dunn.

"It actually was my mistake, after all," admitted Drew. "I ended up apologizing to the checkout clerk. What's weird is that she said some of the same stuff you just said about serving and trying to make things better for others."

Coach Dunn said, "Drew, that lady wasn't just some checkout clerk. She's the restaurant's owner."

"Wait, what? They had like a million people working in there. Why was she still taking our orders and refilling our drinks? What's that all about?" Drew asked.

"As I said, servant leadership," Coach Dunn replied. "It's not about what she can get out of the customers or her employees but rather how can she enrich their lives. Magic Johnson once said, 'ask not what your teammates can do for you but what you can do for your teammates'. When a team is more concerned about each other then they are more likely to go farther together than they could by themselves."

Coach Dunn couldn't believe he was having this conversation with Drew, of all people. Drew tended to be self-focused. He might have been the most gifted basketball player on the team after James and Antonio, but he also knew it and too often, acted the part of a prima donna. The fact that he was still listening and asking questions gave Coach Dunn hope.

"Serving others doesn't mean that you think less of yourself," Coach Dunn continued. "It doesn't mean that you put yourself down. Instead, it means that you think of yourself less. You put the needs of others before your own. In turn, you make their life better, which ultimately will make your life better. You guys share the load. You share the burdens. It's much better to go through life together with friends who have each other's backs rather than worrying about your own agendas."

So far so good, Coach thought. Drew was still paying attention. Coach Dunn didn't know how much longer they'd have a conversation, but he was going to throw out some more nuggets for Drew to consider.

Coach Dunn said, "There was a study done that actually found that we're healthier, both physically and psychologically, when we give to others and help others. It reminds me of the classic song lyrics that say, '*Lean on me when you're not strong. And I'll be your friend, I'll help you carry on. For it won't be long, 'til I'm gonna need somebody to lean on.*'

Antonio and James gave Coach Dunn quite the look as he recited the song lyrics but wisely, didn't offer an opinion on his singing voice.

"As a basketball player, you can volunteer to rebound for a teammate," he continued. "You can go over plays with a teammate. You can work on ball-handling together. You can watch film together. You can hold each other accountable. Keep each other out of trouble.

Find ways to help your teammates be better. This will make you better as well. No matter your age or status in life, you can always help others out. You can lean on each other."

"That's deep coach. But I can respect that," said Drew. "Is that why you sweep the floor and put out all of the cones before practice. I thought we have managers and custodians to do that stuff."

Coach Dunn said, "I try to do whatever helps move our team forward and if I can help out somebody in the process, then I try to do that. As you mentioned, managers and custodians, for example, have a lot of things to do. If I can take something off their plate, then I try to do that. At the end of the day, somebody has to do all of these things. From a traditional way of thinking, I have certainly paid my dues and shouldn't have to do these things, but I just think it's the right thing to do."

Sitting in a nearby seat, Angela was enjoying this conversation. Not only did she want the players to be physically healthy but mentally healthy, as well. She felt that Drew was learning something, and she was glad that Coach Dunn was taking the time to talk with him.

When there was a slight pause in the conversation between Drew and Coach Dunn, Angela said, "Even though I was a biology major, I had to take some business classes. I had this one professor that gave us a test. Before giving the test, the professor said, 'I've taught you everything that I can teach you about business in the last ten weeks, but the most important message or question that I could ask would be what's the name of the lady that cleans this building during the day. That is the only question on this test'. Even though I knew the material from the chapter, I failed that test. I think of that story often. Everybody I come in contact with is important. Everyone has a story. If I can be a small help to them in some way or if I can treat them with kindness in some way, then I'm passing that test so to speak. I figure that if we all help each other then it's like iron sharpening iron. It's like Coach and the old song says about leaning on me when you're not strong."

Coach Dunn added, "I know that every time you scroll through your social media feeds, it seems that you're flooded with negativity. We see people being mean. We see people being selfish. But the world is still full of people doing great things. Gandhi used to say, '*Be the change you want to see in the world*'. Just because other people are negative doesn't mean we have to be. We should be kind to others, not because we get rewarded or because the other person is kind, but because we're kind."

"Absolutely. Coach is right," said Angela. "Martin Luther King, Jr. had a dream that people would be judged by the content of their character. The world still isn't perfect, nor will it ever be. We can't help everyone, but we can help someone. We can't do everything, but we can do something. Instead of throwing up my hands and saying that things are hopeless, I want to be the change I want to see in the world. I want to do what I can do where I'm at."

Coach Dunn looked at Drew and said, "Angela had some great thoughts about helping others. She does that every day as our trainer. I try to be a servant leader as a coach. If that means helping others by putting out cones or even carrying bags, then that is what I want to do. MLK also said that 'It's always the right time to do what it's right'. I figure that it's always the right time to help out a custodian or a manager, or anyone for that matter."

It was quiet and for a moment, Coach Dunn was concerned that he and Angela had gone too far with Drew and lost him.

"Dunn's deep thoughts," Drew said, breaking the silence. "What you guys say makes a lot of sense. Now, I just need to find out the name of our custodian."

The comment eased Coach's fears. He was relieved that Drew was responsive to their talk. Coach smiled and replied, "It's Tom but everyone calls him Woody."

COACH'S FAVORITES

As the bus rolled along the freeway, many of the players were on their phones. Learie was no exception. But unlike his teammates, he was the only one communicating with someone that had confronted Coach Dunn in a negative manner that day.

"You've been pretty quiet all night. You okay?" Brandon asked Learie, his fellow co-captain.

"Just been texting with my dad."

"I saw him and Coach talking in the hallway after the game. Your dad looked kind of mad. What was that all about?"

"Yeah, I guess he got on coach pretty hard and will be talking to him tomorrow sometime. He is going to find out why I'm not playing much. Coach has just had it out for me all year. I just need a chance but I'm not sure he's going to give me any."

"What was the deal tonight? I thought you were going in but then you didn't."

"That wasn't right, man. Coach wanted me to go in and then he told me to go sit back down. Obviously, I ended up not playing even though the game was a blowout. I was the only one not to play. That was embarrassing."

"That stinks. Sorry. Did he say why he changed his mind?"

"He never said a word after the game to me. It's been like that all year. He never gives me a chance. He definitely plays favorites and it's obvious that I'm not one of his favorites."

"I know the season's been tough for you, but do you really think Coach plays favorites?"

"It's obvious. Of course, he does."

"I've got the solution," said Brandon, as if a lightbulb had appeared above his head.

"Oh yeah, what's that?"

"Become one of his favorites. Boom! Problem solved. Next," Brandon remarked with a smile.

"Not quite that simple."

"Why not?"

"Because Coach is set in his ways. It's obvious that he already has his favorites."

"Then how do you explain a couple of weeks ago when he played Scott and he ended up getting like a million rebounds and knocked down a bunch of jumpers? He's even ended up playing quite a bit since then despite being a freshman."

"Right but Scott hit those shots. He got a chance."

"You don't remember when you had a chance around the same time?" asked Brandon.

"I guess, I do. But Coach didn't let me play my game."

"Your game? What are you saying? You got off a bunch of shots and were cold as ice. It was like a community service activity. We could've gathered up all your bricks and built a house for some needy family. I don't remember the last time you got extra shots in or stayed after practice. If your game is to shoot, then you weren't putting yourself in a very good position to make anything."

"Whatever," Learie said dismissively.

"Not whatever. Scott was ready for his opportunity because he worked on his game every day after practice even though he wasn't seeing much action. He still stayed sharp. He gained confidence but maybe, more importantly, Coach also gained confidence in him. Scott wasn't playing much before but now he plays a decent amount. Even when he isn't hitting, he still has Coach's trust because Coach sees how hard he's working."

"Yeah, he's lucky to be one of Coach's favorites now."

"You're right. He's one of Coach's favorites now but that's because he did what coach wanted," Brandon stated.

"Coach always talks about hustling and getting loose balls, but I think that's just talk."

"What do you mean? It seems genuine to me."

"I dove for that loose ball a few weeks ago. That should have shown Coach that I'm serious. He talks a big game, but I didn't get rewarded. In fact, he barely acknowledged me diving for that loose ball. I've also come early to practice a couple of times and he still didn't give me a chance."

"But that's not the right way to look at things. A couple of times isn't enough to earn his trust. You have to do things over and over again until he knows you're serious. It'll also start to become a habit. I saw a post on social media that I thought of when you mentioned loose balls. It said, 'Bad players remember the good things they do but good players remember the times that they messed up'."

"That's one of those things that sounds good, but it doesn't matter. Coach is still going to be against me. Remember that time we both missed practice and you didn't get in trouble, but I did?"

"How could I forget? We were coming back from Christmas break for the first practice and we were riding together. I did actually get in trouble, but just not as much as you. Remember that I had to run some sprints before I could practice?"

"We both had to run, but unlike you, I also got suspended for a game. That wasn't fair," complained Learie

"I don't know about that. Don't you remember when we got to the gym and practice was just getting over? The very first thing out of your mouth was 'my parents didn't wake me up'. No apologies. No nothing but blaming your parents. What are you, 12 years old? Set your own alarm clock."

"Well, I certainly didn't whine and cry for forgiveness like you did," said Learie mimicking a baby.

"I didn't whine quite like that," corrected Brandon. "I just apologized for missing practice. I truly was sorry for that. I was also sorry that it hurt the team's preparation because someone else had to run my spots in practice."

"You were just sorry that it made you look bad."

"Well, that might be true, also. Nobody ever wants to look bad, but that doesn't mean I wasn't sorry."

"I've wondered something about that day. Why didn't you say it was my fault? I was your ride after all," wondered Learie.

"That might be true, but I made the choice to ride with you. I could have called you sooner when I saw that you weren't at my house on time. But the bottom line is it really didn't matter why I missed practice. I missed practice and that wasn't what I was supposed to do."

"Isn't that noble?" said Learie sarcastically.

"Choices and actions have consequences. Sometimes good and sometimes bad. Regardless, of whose fault it was, I didn't do what I was supposed to do. I was supposed to be at practice, but I didn't do that. Sure, I had a good reason for missing practice. My so-called friend was driving me and couldn't get out of bed without his parents waking him up. Talk about being a baby. But none of that matters. At the end of the day, we're responsible for controlling what we can control, and I didn't do that. No reason to try to get out of trouble or pass the buck. I just decided to own up to it and accept the consequences."

"Accept the consequences? You didn't have to do much compared to me," complained Learie again.

"You keep saying that and it might be true that your consequences were worse but remember I accepted responsibility and didn't give excuses," Brandon pointed out to Learie. "You were full of excuses and didn't accept responsibility. Besides, you had missed a couple of other practices right before Christmas break that was probably still on Coach's mind."

"Those were to take some tests. Academics first, right?" said Learie.

"Academics first, if appropriate. I know why you were taking those tests. Those were re-tests the professor let you make up because you slept through the regular tests. I guess academics weren't first when it came to sleep. I also know that you suggested our practice times as when you could take the makeup tests. That way you could get out of practice. I heard you use that academics-first stuff on Coach when you told him you couldn't be at practice. I don't think you fooled him, but I guess he wasn't going to fight you on it."

"All of this might be true to a degree, but Coach still hasn't told me why he's not playing me more or giving me a chance in games," said Learie.

"Don't you know what you need to do? You're not in junior pro anymore. You know what is right and wrong for basketball players to do. Does coach really need to spell it out for you?" asked Brandon.

Learie got defensive and responded very quickly, "He should. He should be letting me know how I can get more playing time! What does he think? Does he think I like sitting on the bench?"

"Have you asked him?" wondered Brandon

"I actually did back in the fall and he just basically ignored me."

"He did? That's a little surprising."

"He said I asked the wrong question. He said he understood everybody wants more playing time but that is a selfish question.

Being consumed with playing time when you're part of a team is selfish. He said that the better question would be to ask how I can improve so that the team can improve. Yeah, that pretty much ended that discussion."

"Actually, that sounds like it could have led to a longer conversation. That could have been the opening you needed to find out more about how a senior co-captain could help the team when he's not playing," suggested Brandon.

"No, it just showed me that he wasn't concerned about my playing time," Learie snapped back.

"You're probably right about that," admitted Brandon. "Coach probably doesn't care who exactly is getting playing time. He's most likely worried about the entire team. He wants the team to be as good as possible. Let me ask you a question."

"Fire away," said Learie.

"When Coach yells at us after a game about turning the ball over too many times, what are you thinking?" asked Brandon.

"I'm wondering why he played those players if they turn the ball over so much."

"What about when we get out-rebounded and he says we're being lazy?" asked Brandon.

"I'm wondering why he didn't put somebody else in the game if he was so upset about the effort."

"How many games do we have in a year?"

"25 or 30," answered Learie.

"How many practices, workouts, and training sessions do we have?"

"Seems like they never end. Hundreds!" exclaimed Learie.

"Right," said Brandon. "Coach is probably more likely to believe what he sees repeatedly in practice than in just one game. If the players he trusts are turning the ball over or not putting forth the effort, he might give them a little extra leeway because he sees them doing something else in practice.

Speaking of leeway, it seemed to Brandon that Learie wasn't getting upset but instead was allowing him to ask questions, so Brandon continued.

"What do you think would happen if the days following a game when Coach is mad because we got outrebounded, that you dominate the boards or make tons of hustle plays?"

"Coach would probably notice," admitted Learie.

"Exactly and then you'd be on your way to being one of his favorites," said Brandon. "Coach tells us all the time what being one of his favorites looks like. You don't have to guess or listen hard even though he doesn't come right out and say it. When he mentions that the team isn't hustling, he is looking for someone to hustle. If he puts up the free throw stats of everybody in the league or mentions this constantly, then he values good free throw shooters. If he makes a big deal of the academic honor players, then going to class is important. Whatever he talks about the most is what he values. Give that to him. That is how you become his favorite."

"I've seen coaches that it just doesn't matter, though," said Learie

"There are probably coaches like that out there, but typically we're seeing things only from our perspective. Remember, in high school when I was upset with my baseball coach because I was platooning and not batting as high up in the order as I wanted?" asked Brandon.

"I do. Did you ever talk with the coach?"

"I didn't. But my mom came to see him. She told him that I had more hits than so and so player and so she couldn't understand why I wasn't getting more of an opportunity because I was clearly a better hitter. He proceeded to show her how the other kid actually had a way better on-base percentage, fielding percentage, and had more hustle plays. Even though he was going to be out, he still ran out way more fly balls and ground outs than I did. That wasn't even something that I thought the coach was paying attention to, let alone keeping stats on. He told my mom that I had potential but was too focused on things I couldn't control. Instead of worrying about playing time, or spot in the order, I should be hustling more, taking more fielding practice, and taking more walks instead of swinging at everything. After that conversation, I didn't complain any longer. My mom told me that she was never going to confront a coach again getting only one side of the story."

"Interesting story about your mom. I didn't know that. I guess talking about parents brings us full-circle back to my dad and him confronting Coach Dunn," said Learie.

T-SHIRT

What might be unusual for some was commonplace for Brandon and Learie. Deep conversations might be avoided by many but not these guys. The life-long friends had been there for each other through the good times and bad times of growing up, and they weren't afraid to tackle some tough issues along the way.

"Which brings us back to your dad," repeated Brandon. "Have you been totally straight with him about your missed practices, questionable attitude, and constant excuses?"

"Dude, if you weren't my brother from another mother, I'd probably punch you right now," said Learie.

The Eagles' co-captains looked at each other for a brief moment as they considered the conversation they had been having.

"If we weren't close, I wouldn't be telling you this," responded Brandon. "I care about you and want you to do well. I also care about our team and want the team to do well. If you do better, then the team can do better. I also know from the situation with my mom and the high school baseball team that we sometimes only see our side of things. Sometimes, we only see our tree and not the whole forest."

"You know you sound like Jaylen, right?" said Learie as he thought about his roommate and some of the late-night conversations they had through the years. "He says some of this stuff sometimes. He doesn't bang me over the head with it like you are right now, but he gets his little digs in. Have you two been talking about me or my situation behind my back?

"Nope, but because Jaylen is your roommate, he cares about you. You and I have been tight since we were kids. You know I have your back, which is why I have to speak up. I know that you feel wronged and I know that you think it's coach's fault but you might be a little too consumed with that and putting your energy there instead of putting your energy toward things you can control."

Brandon paused for a moment, squinting his eyes, and smiling as he looked at the shirt that Learie was wearing.

"I know that we think Coach is a little cheesy sometimes with his clichés or sayings. We probably haven't even given much thought to it but look at the shirts that we're all wearing. Yes, even you. You're wearing our team shirt that says 'excUses'. Have you ever thought about that? The 'u' is bigger than the other letters. What's in the middle of all excuses? You are. We're. When we make excuses, we're the reason. We're in the middle of them. We're not taking responsibility for things. Do you remember when we had that hard rain our senior year of football for homecoming?"

Even though it was painful at the time, Learie now laughed at the memory.

"How could I forget that monsoon."

"Yeah, we got upset by like four touchdowns in our homecoming game," said Brandon. "All we could talk about afterward was that if it hadn't been raining so hard, we'd have killed that team. It took me a while, but it finally dawned on me one day that they also played on that same wet field with the same wet ball. The conditions were the same for them as they were for us. We just didn't react well. We had penalties. Passes were dropped. We slipped instead of getting low or sitting down in our cuts. I remember that halftime was full of excuses and that just led us to play worse in the second half."

"I never thought of that," said Learie.

"I love these t-shirts that coach got us. Every time I see them, I think about the excuses I've made in my life. I can't remember a single time that an excuse has gotten me closer to a goal that I had. Last summer, I saw this Navy SEALS documentary and it also inspired me to eliminate excuses. I decided that if something is important, I will find a way to get it done. If it's not important then I will find an excuse. I think excuses are for people who don't want something bad enough."

"Alright! Seriously, enough. I get it. I'm a bad person, who always has an excuse on standby," said a frustrated Learie.

"You're not a bad person. I'm your friend and I just want to see you take responsibility for the things you can control. You'll be much happier that way."

"Happier?!? You know how I'd be happier?" asked Learie with a smile.

"By taking responsibility for your actions?"

"Well, there is that but, no. I was thinking that if I had a few more dollars in my pocket like those rich tech guys, then that would make me happy!"

"I think we'd all be happier if we had more money. Way to change the subject on me."

"You noticed that, huh?" said a smiling Learie.

"Sure did. Speaking of those rich guys, though," said Brandon. "Did you know that a few years ago, Amazon ordered something like four thousand pink iPods from Apple for Christmas? As it turned out, Apple couldn't fulfill the order in time for Christmas. This was not good for Amazon because they had already sold all of those to their customers and were just waiting for Apple to send them to Amazon. What would you have done in that situation?"

"I probably would have just apologized to my customers that were silly enough to buy a pink iPod," answered Learie.

"That might have been what I'd have done, also. Not because they were pink or any other color but because it wasn't our fault that they weren't available."

"Exactly. It wasn't Amazon's fault."

"You're right. It wasn't their fault, but Amazon believed that it was completely their responsibility to do what they could do to make the situation right. What Amazon did reminds me of how we should be approaching basketball or anything else. They took responsibility for something that happened."

"Oh, here we go," joked Learie.

"Yes, here we go again. Just because you tried to change the subject earlier, doesn't mean that I'm done with you."

"Okay, I give in," said Learie. "How did Amazon take responsibility for Apple's mess up?"

"Amazon figured that people didn't care about why or what happened. People just wanted the stuff that they ordered," Brandon continued. "If you advertise it, then you should have it. Amazon literally went out to stores and bought pink iPods at the retail cost. They repackaged these brand-new iPods in Amazon packaging and then sent them out to all of the customers that had preordered them."

"I bet that killed their profit margin."

"Definitely but they figured they can make excuses, or they can be the best, but they can't be both. True champions find ways to get done what needs to be done. Amazon was willing to take a loss on an item because they were ultimately responsible for what they offered on their site. Instead of making excuses and giving lame explanations, they just found a way to get things done."

"Yes, yes, yes. I get it. Be responsible. Quit making excuses. Remember what's on the front of my team t-shirt. I get it," exclaimed Learie.

"And they said you were hard-headed. I don't think that's the case at all. You aren't a bad person. You'll actually listen to reason after all."

"Ha ha ha!"

Learie laughed in a mocking tone but it was obvious that he was joking around with his fellow co-captain.

"By the way," Learie continued. "The reason Coach made me sit back down on the bench…"

"You said you didn't know," responded Brandon.

"That's not entirely true," confessed Learie. "I asked him which player he wanted me to guard."

"That sounds like a good question. I don't see how that should've been a problem."

"It might've been a good question at the appropriate time. But just like academics first in the appropriate time that we were talking about earlier, it wasn't a good time."

"I don't quite follow. Why was it a bad time?" Brandon asked.

"My question was right after the timeout when he told us that we were in the Blitz for the rest of the game, no matter what. I wasn't paying attention at all during the timeout. I was actually complaining to Demetrius that it didn't look like I was going to play in that game, either," admitted Learie. "Hashtag, oops."

"That makes more sense now. You've got to tell your dad that. In fact, you probably need to level with him about a bunch of stuff when it comes to your playing time. Tell him that you are going to do better and become one of Coach's favorites. Tell him that he doesn't need to talk with Coach yet because you haven't taken care of your business yet. You haven't controlled what you can control."

"In other words," said Learie with a smirk. "Tell my dad that I'm going to do my best to become more like Jaylen in how he leads and performs."

"Whatever works."

Brandon looked up at the TV monitor above his seat and then back over to Learie.

"Good talk. You know I want to help you and all. I feel that I've kind of accomplished that mission tonight. But I've got to be honest with you. I can't be this serious much longer. It was a good talk and you've got a lot to think about. We've been serious for quite a while. I either need to take a mental break from being your shrink, or I need to get paid. Since you're broke, I think I'll this break time to watch this game on TV."

Learie looked at his long-time friend and just shook his head. It had been a good talk and he had a lot to think about. He didn't expect this tonight, but it could prove to be an important conversation. Learie's thoughts were interrupted by Brandon and his parting wisdom.

"Maybe you should think about texting your dad back and letting him know that you'll call him at the next stop. I'm guessing that you have a few things to discuss with him."

TRUCK STOP

M r. Frank brought the bus to a complete stop in front of the truck stop, so it was a short walk, especially for Jaylen and his crutches.

"Remember to have your travel suits on and to represent our school and yourselves in a first-class manner when we go into this truck stop," insisted Coach Dunn.

Mr. Frank added, "We'll be rolling out in 30 minutes, so please plan accordingly."

The players headed many different directions as they got off the bus. Some went to use the restrooms. Some went to get food or snacks. But most of them raced to find a good place to plug in their phone chargers and breathe new life into their most prized possessions.

Demetrius and Bobbi found a great outlet right next to some very comfy seats. They were relieved because they wouldn't have to stand for the entire thirty minutes that they were at the truck stop.

"My mom gave me one of these power banks for Christmas and it has been a lifesaver, at least as far as my phone is concerned. Sure, I'll be charging up my phone while we wait but I don't really have to. I'm always prepared if I run out of juice. I have this little portable phone charger with me at all times," said Bobbi.

"I probably should get one of those, myself," Demetrius responded back to his roommate.

"It'd be a good idea. Never can be too prepared when it comes to your phone's battery. If my battery died, I don't know what I'd do. I imagine if your battery was dead, or almost dead, and we didn't stop somewhere that had outlets, you'd be hurting."

"True story," agreed Demetrius.

"Speaking of being prepared, Coach Dunn might not have realized this, but in the game today, there were a few times where the guy you were guarding did simple things to get around you," said Bobbi.

"I'm pretty sure Coach noticed that."

"He probably did notice but he probably didn't know why it happened," corrected Bobbi. "What I meant was that each of those times I remember, it was something from our scouting report. You could have probably stopped them if you knew what their tendencies were. I'm guessing Coach just assumed you knew the scouting report. But I know different. I know that you didn't pay attention to that stuff or go over it at all. It came back to bite us."

"Well, I didn't quite expect Jaylen to get hurt. I obviously wasn't expecting to be called into action," confessed Demetrius.

"We got manhandled pretty bad tonight against a team that we probably should have beaten. I don't know if it would have made a difference, but you had a chance to play and you weren't ready and that showed. At least to me, it showed. Every time you allowed your man to score, it made it that much more difficult for us to generate any momentum or mount a comeback."

"I didn't really think about it from a team perspective," admitted Demetrius. "My bad."

"That's why I'm saying something," said Bobbi. "Look, I certainly don't always do what I'm supposed to do but I try to be prepared. I don't have your athleticism but if I can think quicker. If I can be prepared and be a step ahead of our opponents mentally then I might be able to make up for my lack of athletic ability. I want to try and finish the year strong and there is no way that is going to happen if we're not prepared. It's more important than ever now that Jaylen is hurt."

"I hear you. I just don't believe it's going to be worth it all the time. I'm not sure I want to take the time to prepare and then not play."

"You might not be getting the chances you want from Coach. It also might not be worth it from your perspective. But if you aren't prepared and then fail when given the opportunity, do you think you'll get that chance again?" asked Bobbi.

Demetrius just looked at Bobbi. In some ways, he was hoping that Bobbi was finished but he also knew that Bobbi usually had a good perspective on things.

Bobbi continued, "You'll probably just be proving that coach is right by not playing you. I know that you don't like the fact that you aren't playing and that leads you to not care but it actually becomes a vicious cycle that not only hurts you but the team also. You're mad that you aren't playing so you choose not to prepare. Then, you finally get a chance but aren't prepared, so you do poorly. This causes Coach to not play you anymore and then you have a bad attitude again."

"Thanks, Socrates!" joked Demetrius. I can tell you are paying attention in your Intro to Philosophy course."

"Now that you mention it, I'm reminded of one of my favorite philosophers and literary scholars."

"Oh yeah, who's that?" inquired Demetrius.

"Captain Jack Sparrow from Pirates of the Caribbean, of course," said a smirking Bobbi. "Captain Jack said that the problem is not the problem but that the problem is your attitude toward the problem."

"Deep. Real deep."

"Make jokes all you want but it's true," Bobbi responded. "Not playing stinks, but you still get opportunities once in a while. The real problem is your attitude toward not playing. That leads you to not be prepared. If tonight was a really close game and you got to play, you could have been the X-factor one way or another. You would have played poorly because of being unprepared, which could have kept us from winning a close game. On the flip side, think if you had been prepared and were called into action in a close game. Combine your preparation with your athletic ability and you could have been the difference maker and helped propel us to victory."

"But it wasn't a close game."

"Absolutely, but you don't always know what the situation will be. You just have to train and prepare for when your opportunity comes. Don't worry about the situation. Just be prepared. If you were prepared tonight, we probably wouldn't have won because it was such a large margin but remember we came back twice last year from bigger margins against better teams, so you never really know."

"I guess so," Demetrius said somewhat dismissively.

"You guess so, but I know so! It reminds me of what the Navy SEALs say."

"I know, I know," Demetrius interrupted. "The only easy day was yesterday."

"Well, that is a great quote, but it wasn't what I was going to say."

"By all means, continue my young but wise philosopher."

"I actually thought of another one just now as you were mocking me. The Navy SEALs say 'The more you sweat in training, the less you'll bleed in battle' but that wasn't the one that I originally thought about. The one I really like is 'Under pressure you don't rise to the occasion but instead sink to the level of your training'."

"I guess those make sense."

"You bet they make sense," said Bobbi. "Today you had the opportunity to play. But, no matter how badly you may have wanted to do well, you weren't going to be your best. More importantly, you weren't going to be what our team needed. You could have tried to rise to the occasion but it would matter because you weren't ready. You didn't have it in you to be at your best. You couldn't rise to the occasion because you hadn't prepared."

Demetrius thought about this for a moment and it was like a lightbulb came on above his head.

"My grandpa used to say something weird that I just thought about as you were talking. He used to use an Abe Lincoln quote. I guess honest Abe would say that if he had six hours to cut down a tree, he'd spend the first four hours sharpening the blade."

"That's cool. I hadn't heard that one before," said Bobbi. "I wasn't a Boy Scout and I don't know how to tie those cool fancy knots, but their motto is 'Always be Prepared'. I think if we did a little more of that, then we'd be ready for our opportunities when they come our way."

Just then, Mr. Frank approached the two players as they were talking at the truck stop.

OPPORTUNITY KNOCKS

M r. Frank had refilled his coffee tumbler and was walking out when he saw the two roommates talking. He was always impressed by how Bobbi and Demetrius could be very different from one another but still demonstrate mutual respect. Though they had only been roommates since the beginning of the school year, they had a special friendship that allowed for some tough conversations, much like Brandon and Learie.

"I couldn't help but hear some of your fellas' conversation," he said. "You know, I have found that for much of my life, the harder I prepared the luckier I seemed to get. I think that success can occur when opportunity meets preparation. Sure, there are times when we prepare and that opportunity that we so desperately want never actually comes to us. But I'd much rather be prepared just in case. I'm not sure I'd want to live with the regret of knowing that something was right there in front of me, but I wasn't ready."

Neither of the players could argue with that. It made sense to both of them.

"You fellas ever heard of Wally Pipp?" asked Mr. Frank.

"No," the two players said in unison.

"You ever heard of Lou Gehrig?"

"There's a disease with that name, right?" asked Bobbi.

"That's right. The disease is actually ALS and it attacks the nerve cells and your muscles," said Mr. Frank. "Lou Gehrig's life was cut short because of this disease and so it's commonly referred to as Lou Gehrig's disease. But Lou Gehrig was also a baseball player way back in the day. In fact, he was the backup to this fella named Wally Pipp. One day Wally Pipp got sick and wasn't able to play and so Gehrig finally got his chance."

"Once again, I feel some kind of lesson coming from you Mr. Frank. I'm guessing Lou Gehrig was either really prepared or wasn't prepared at all. So, which was it?" asked Bobbi.

"Oh, Gehrig was definitely prepared. In fact, he played so well that Wally Pipp never got his starting spot back. Lou Gehrig played so well that he actually played in every game for the New York Yankees for the next 13 years! Despite being sick at various times and suffering 17 fractures in his hands during his career, he never missed a game for 2,130 straight games. He held that record for more than 50 years until Cal Ripken, Jr. came along and broke it."

Demetrius and Bobbi were amazed at that story. Thirteen straight years and never missing a game was incredible and it all started because one guy got sick and another guy was ready.

"Yessiree. Gehrig was more than ready for his chance. I know that is a story about the olden days, but we see these things play out all the time. We saw this with Nick Foles winning a Super Bowl as the backup quarterback for the Philadelphia Eagles. We saw this with that fella at Alabama that came off the bench to quarterback the Crimson Tide to a championship. We saw Ohio State win a national championship in football with their third-string quarterback. You've got to be ready to answer the door when opportunity knocks."

"Mr. Frank, you really like football, don't you?" asked Demetrius. "It seems you're always talking about football."

"Sure do. I played a little halfback myself in college. I like to use football stories and analogies, but you can find lots of stories like these from all different sports. Unfortunately, there are more stories about players who got a chance and they weren't ready. The sad reality is you don't usually hear about them. You just look back and wonder why such and such team didn't fulfill its' potential. Since you fellas are basketball players, here's a basketball story that just came to my mind."

As a deep thinker and a philosophy major, Bobbi loves to hear good stories. Maybe, more importantly, he was excited because he was hoping Mr. Frank would deliver a lesson that would speak to his roommate Demetrius and go along with what Bobbi had been trying to tell him.

"I was vacationing in the OBX, you know, the Outer Banks of North Carolina when I heard this story. It was all over the news," said Mr. Frank. "North Carolina won the national championship in 2017, but history almost told a different story. The Tarheels needed a game-winning shot from a former walk-on in the Elite Eight game to advance. Amazingly that former walk-on, Luke Maye, was only averaging about five points per game and was only playing about 15 minutes per game. He was something like the eighth-leading scorer on the team. They were playing Kentucky in that game and the Wildcats didn't focus on him during the last possession. I don't blame them. Luke Maye was the least likely guy on the court to become a hero. But, wouldn't you know. That fella knocked down his wide-open jumper and the rest is history."

"That is amazing," said Demetrius. "I didn't know that."

"A lot of people loved that story because he was a former walk-on, but that wasn't all there was to the story. The reason I tell you, fellas, that story is because his coach would say later that Luke was always practicing and preparing for a moment like this even though it was unlikely to ever come."

There it was. That was the lesson Bobbi had been hoping for. It seemed that Demetrius was listening intently to Mr. Frank's story and it had to have touched a nerve.

"Thanks for sharing, Mr. Frank. I probably need to do a better job of preparing myself, especially if my goal is to be a hero and get all the publicity, right?" Demetrius said with a big grin.

"Yeah, thanks Mr. Frank," Bobbi added.

"You're very welcome, fellas. Just remember that everybody wants to be a champion but not everyone is willing to prepare to be a champion. Now, with all of that said, hopefully, your cell phones are charged because it's about time to get back on the road. As the Bandit says, 'we've got a long way to go and a short time to get there'."

"The Bandit?" asked Demetrius as he checked to see how much charge his phone now had.

"You know, Burt Reynolds from Smokey and the Bandit. It's a classic. My grandson absolutely loves it, but we have to keep telling him that it's not good to run from the cops even though Burt Reynolds looks cool doing it. We have to remind my grandson it's just a movie. It's just entertainment. Anyway, I know that you don't really care about all of that or an old movie, so we probably need to go get loaded up."

The guys watched Mr. Frank walk out the door.

"That Mr. Frank is really wise," Bobbi pointed out.

"Yeah, but really old," added Demetrius. "I never heard of that movie."

"He might be really old, but I guess we're really young. We don't know it all."

"Wait, what?!?" said a smiling Demetrius.

"We don't know it all, but I get the sneaky suspicion we might start knowing more. The more we prepare, the more we'll know and that just might give us the edge we need."

"I'm going to use the bathroom and get a drink and then I'll meet you on the bus, but I want to let you know that you've inspired me. That is, you and Mr. Frank, but I'm now convinced that I've got to be prepared. I need to be ready. When opportunity knocks, I need to be ready to answer the door."

"Awesome to hear," responded Bobbi. "Now, hurry up so you get on the bus before Antonio and James!"

DR. WILSON'S CLASS

It hadn't been very long since the guys had been at the truck stop. Normally after a pit stop like that, everyone is wide awake and talkative. Tonight, was no exception, but some of the players had tests coming up that they needed to prepare for.

"Hey Brandon, are you going to play cards with us in a few minutes?" asked Chaz.

"I don't think I'll be able to, thanks. I have a bunch of homework to get done."

"Oh, my goodness, what a nerd!" Chaz joked.

"True story but probably one of us should see an 'A' at some point in our lives," Brandon snapped back.

"Okay, okay, haha, everyone's a comedian. You know this college thing wouldn't be so bad if we didn't have to go to class."

"Yes, and mornings wouldn't be so bad if they were later in the day."

At this point, Brandon's roommate Matt decided to chime in and get in on the banter.

"Or, as my Papi used to say, 'if ifs and buts were candy and nuts, every day would be a holiday'," said Matt.

Even though Matt was a year behind Brandon in school, they had roomed together ever since Brandon hosted Matt on a recruiting visit.

Matt had been a solid player so far in his three years with the Eagles. He was well-liked and had a good sense of humor. He would be a fine captain next year when he was a senior and his roommate had graduated.

"Seriously though, you know I'm not much for school, but Dr. Wilson's class is my favorite," said Chaz. "When I was in elementary school, my dad would pick me up and he'd ask me what my favorite thing was about the day and I would always say recess. Well, not always. Sometimes, I would say lunch."

"That's deep. Thanks so much for sharing something so personal," Matt snarked.

"Anyway, like I was saying Dr. Wilson is cool and his class is tolerable," Said Chaz

"Tolerable? That's some high praise coming from you," said Matt.

"It is what it is."

Dr. Daniel Wilson was a very popular teacher at their school. He taught a lot of Physical Education and Kinesiology classes and had a special way of connecting with the students and making his material relevant. Not only did he teach about the world of sports, but always tried to tie it in with life, as well. Many of the athletes liked taking his classes because he wasn't boring and kept them engaged.

"Do you remember last week in class when we were talking about facilities and getting stadiums and arenas ready for games?" asked Matt. "It's crazy how quickly they can transform an ice hockey rink into a basketball court and all that goes into getting the grass and the field ready for baseball and football games when those teams have grass," said Matt.

Chaz added, "What stood out to me was the fact that nobody ever knows who those people are. They also get paid very little, relatively speaking, and yet they have some of the most important jobs of anyone in the organization in order for that game to be played. I know you need players to play a game, but those millionaires don't play if the field or court isn't ready."

"I liked the field trip he took us on last week," said Matt. "It was awesome to see how it all works for an NBA organization."

"That was awesome," agreed Chaz. "Were you as surprised as I was in how much pride those people had in working for that organization? Even though they were getting paid nothing compared to their bosses sitting at desks, or certainly the players, they still enjoyed their work and knew that it mattered."

"That was a little unexpected," said Matt.

"After that field trip, Dr. Wilson actually brought that up to some of us. He said they were constantly reminding themselves of how important their work was. They worked as a team to make the game possible for the real team that everybody knows."

Matt nodded his head in agreement saying, "It was funny how we were supposed to be learning about the nuts and bolts of operating a facility and yet Dr. Wilson found a way to talk about life and team and all that stuff."

"He even told that story about the old Navy pilot way back that got shot down. Mr. Frank probably knows the story since it's an old story," said Chaz playfully.

Despite the fact he was trying to do his homework, Brandon was still half-listening to their conversation. Brandon had never had Dr. Wilson for a class but heard that he was a good teacher.

"My uncle was a Navy pilot," said Brandon. "What was the story Dr. Wilson told you guys in class?"

"This hotshot Navy fighter pilot finally got shot down after 75 successful missions but survived because he parachuted out. Years later, he's at a restaurant and this guy comes up to him and introduces himself. The pilot doesn't know who he is but apparently, this guy knows the pilot. Turns out that guy packed the pilot's parachute that day," Matt recalled.

"No way!" said Brandon.

"Dr. Wilson told us that story to emphasize even though we may have a role that seems insignificant, that it can still be very important.

It may not be life or death like this parachute packer and pilot, but it can still be crucial," said Matt.

"Like my theater teacher my sophomore year always said, 'there are no small parts, only small actors'," added Brandon.

"That reminds me that I have to take some kind of performing arts or music class still," said Chaz. "I'm not looking forward to that. I wish I could just play basketball."

"Or go to recess all the time," Matt said with a smile.

"At least I know you were listening to me," said Chaz.

"That pilot story was interesting to me," said Matt. "I'm glad that Dr. Wilson shared it with us. He said that on all teams, whether it's in sports, or a family, or in business, what one person does affects everybody else. He said that we typically think it only matters what the star does not the other players. He also said that most people think the term 'role player' is a dirty phrase. That it's an insult, but it's just a matter of perspective. A role player is just someone that is playing a particular role. Steph Curry can be a role player."

Matt could tell by the look on Chaz's face that he was a little confused as to how an all-star like Steph Curry could be a role player.

"On some plays, Steph Curry is supposed to shoot. On some plays, he is supposed to set screens. On other plays, he might need to make passes. His role depends on what the team needs," added Matt.

"But isn't being labeled a role player kind of degrading? It's like you don't have any talent," wondered Chaz.

"That isn't the way we have to look at it," said Matt. "A role player has a bunch of talent. Their talent is in that role they are playing. The parachute packer might not have been able to fly a jet, but he could pack a mean parachute. That talent ended up saving the pilot's life. If we're a true team, then we want people that help one another out and complement each other. If you have a team full of shooters but no one is willing to set screens, then it might be difficult to get open shots and the team will suffer."

"I guess it's all about your perspective," said Chaz.

Matt nodded in agreement with Chaz's comment and then further explained his thoughts on roles.

"You're right Chaz. If our perspective or our focus is centered on us or were focused on getting recognized in the newspaper or on TV, then we probably don't want to be known as a role player in a traditional sense. I'll tell you what though, being a role player is extremely valuable to the team. If I'm a star, then I want people around me that are willing to embrace their roles and be a star in their roles. If I'm a running back, then I need to treat my offensive linemen well. Those big nasties up front are going to create the holes that I run through. We're all in this together. If we're not all doing our jobs, then we don't all experience success. I once heard it said that it takes ten hands to make a basket. Everybody on the court or on the field has to help one another out."

"I never really thought about that from either perspective. I've always just figured stars are stars and everyone else is just a role player," said Chaz.

"Right, but 'just a role player' as you say, can mean so many things," said Matt. "Remember that a star can actually be a role player on a particular play. Like I said earlier, even Steph Curry might have to pass or screen on a play. If he acts like a prima donna or doesn't want to star in this so-called lesser role then that could cost his team. It could also cost him a chance to accomplish his goal of winning a championship."

Despite needing to study, Brandon was having trouble concentrating on his work. The conversation between Matt and Chaz were interesting to the Senior co-captain, as he thought of a story that would fit right into what they were talking about in regard to player roles.

MOST VALUABLE
TEAMMATE

Brandon re-entered the conversation between Chaz and Matt. He had a story of his own that would highlight the importance of all roles on a team.

"I played with a guy named Jordin back in high school. Though he was talented, he wasn't the star scorer. He did the dirty work. He made the hustle plays. He scored when the opportunity presented itself, but he worked really hard to be the glue on our team. In the playoffs our senior year, Jordin had four fouls with one minute to go in a tie game. He was playing help-side defense when my man broke my ankles, left me in the dust, and drove down the lane. Jordin instinctively came over and helped. He took the charge and, in the process, gave us all the momentum. That was a turning point in the game. There's a chance the game could have gone into overtime and we would have needed Jordin. He didn't consider the fact that the refs had been bad the whole game and that this could have been his fifth foul. He didn't shy away from doing what he needed to do. He played his role and took the charge. We won the game and then went on to win the next two and claim the state championship. I wouldn't have gotten a ring if not for Jordin. He played his role and because of it, we were all champions."

"That's a cool story. I never knew that," said his roommate Matt.

"Unfortunately, I also played with another guy who missed out on some big-time scholarships in football," said Brandon. "This guy was a wide receiver and he thought catching footballs was his only role. When the play would be a run play, he wouldn't be in the same stance or come off the line like he did when it was a pass play and there was a chance he'd get the ball. Not only did good defenses catch on to this but so did college recruiters. Many of the top schools backed off him because they didn't like what they saw out of him when he had to play the role of teammate, blocker, or decoy."

Shaking his head, Chaz said, "Stinks to be him."

"Yes, but it also stunk to be his teammates because you are left to wonder how much better they could have been and how many more games the team might have won if he had been a star in all of his roles, not just the one that he wanted?" said Brandon.

"Makes sense," said Matt. "It's like the parachute packer. I bet that guy probably didn't grow up wanting to have that job."

"No, he probably wanted to be one of those Top Gun pilots with the cool sunglasses and all the dates," added Chaz.

"He probably had many days where he felt that the work he was doing was under-appreciated," said Matt. "He probably thought that his role wasn't very important."

"From what you guys said, his role turned out to be very important, like life-and-death important," added Brandon.

"No kidding," agreed Chaz.

Even though he should have been focusing more on his homework, Brandon continued to enjoy the conversation. This was stuff that Chaz needed to hear as he had been struggling with playing a specific role on the team. Chaz was called upon to be a defender and rebounder. Very few plays were called for him.

Brandon said, "That pilot has to be glad that the parachute packer didn't just go through the motions that day. Lucky for the pilot, that the parachute packer chose to be a star in his role, at least on that day."

"When I hear that story, I think of David Ross," said Matt. "Brandon, I know that you were also a big-time baseball player in high school. Have you heard of David Ross?"

"Yeah, he's a coach or manager, right?

"He is now, but he gained his fame as a baseball player," said Matt. "Actually, he was a below-average baseball player, at least from a stats perspective."

"What do you mean by that? Either you're a good player or not, right?" asked Chaz.

"That's not always the case," said Matt. "Just like we talked about with role players starring in their roles and being valuable members of the team, it was like that with David Ross. Like I said, statistically, he wasn't very good. He was probably never his team's Most Outstanding Player, but he certainly was their MVT. Their Most Valuable Teammate."

"Did you just make that up?" asked Chaz

"Maybe, but it works doesn't it?"

"Sure. Now, why was David Ross his team's 'MVT', as you say?"

Matt continued with his story, "Twice during his career, Ross was one of the most sought-after free agents in all of baseball, despite having a .229 batting average and ripping only 106 dingers in his 15-year career."

Brandon's ears perked up as he heard those below-average statistics.

"How in the world was he sought after if he couldn't hit for power, or hit at all, for that matter?" asked Brandon.

"He had an amazing ability to inspire his teammates and make teams better," responded Matt. "Even though he was a backup for most of his career, he got paid. He also got himself two World Series rings, one with the 2013 Red Sox and one with the 2016 Cubs."

"Not too shabby for a role player," said Chaz.

"You're right. In fact, he got carried off the field after Game 7 of the 2016 World Series," said Matt. "He became the oldest player to ever hit a home run in a World Series game. My family were long-suffering Cubs fans, so I remember this like it was yesterday. His Game 7 home run essentially won the game and the series for the Cubs. First World Series Championship in 108 years. Remember, this was a guy that only had 108 home runs in 15 years of playing and he hits one on the biggest stage in the most pressure-packed situation."

"I guess he was ready for his opportunity," said Chaz.

"He was, but he wouldn't even have gotten that opportunity if he didn't embrace his role as a team leader regardless of his position or status," said Matt. "Ross knew he was signed by both the Red Sox and Cubs to be a great teammate, mentor, and backup. He accepted that and it led to him getting two rings on his fingers. He was never an all-star, but I'd say he was a Hall of Fame teammate."

"I didn't know that about him but it's a great story," said Brandon. "There are probably other stories like that from all sports emphasizing the importance of being a star in a role."

Matt agreed with his roommate, "Yep. I imagine that the best teams are made up of players that want to star in their roles, regardless of what those roles are. The best teams help each other and pick up the slack for one another. The best teams don't care who gets the credit. They celebrate successes together. They overcome challenges together. They win and lose together. They make sure that all the jobs and roles are filled regardless of who has to do them."

"Dr. Wilson would be proud that you guys talked about him and his class so much tonight", said Brandon.

"Maybe we should push for this conversation to be counted as extra credit," suggested Matt.

"I don't think that will work, Matt, but I like the way you think," said Chaz with a smile.

TV PRESS CONFERENCE

The bus was equipped with plenty of large monitors allowing every player to have a premium view of the big game being broadcasted tonight.

Similar to many of his teammates, Chaz loved to watch all sports and was particularly excited about the football game that was on the monitors. He was providing non-stop chatter, which Antonio and James couldn't avoid since they were sitting nearby.

"This game's been awesome," said Chaz. "It's been back and forth the whole time, just like they predicted."

"It's been fun to watch even though I'd preferred to have heard more of the announcers than you," Antonio said to Chaz.

"What can I say? I just get excited watching good football, especially when it's the Eagles, baby!"

James and Antonio looked at each other and rolled their eyes.

Chaz continued to talk, "Did you happen to see that graphic they showed talking about the 2018 and 2019 Super Bowl Champions?"

"No, I missed it. Sorry," Antonio said. "It probably said that Tom Brady is the greatest, blah, blah, blah, yadda, yadda, yadda?"

"Don't be a hater. He's the GOAT!" Chaz exclaimed.

"Okay, I'll bite," Antonio said. "What'd that graphic say?"

"It mentioned how the 2018 Eagles Super Bowl championship team and the 2019 Patriots Super Bowl Championship team didn't have a single 1,000-yard rusher or 1,000-yard receiver. Neither one did. In fact, the Eagles had a backup quarterback lead them through the playoffs and to the championship." Said Chaz.

Antonio acknowledged that statistic. "Pretty impressive," he said.

Matt was almost as big of a fan as Chaz was and so he decided to enter the conversation.

"I think they were trying to make the point that the best teams are not always made up of the best individual talent. They showed another statistic that blew my mind. When the Patriots won in 2019, more than half of the NFL's top rushers and top receivers played on teams that missed the playoffs. In other words, as good as Julio Jones was, he couldn't lead his team to the playoffs, even though he led the NFL in receiving yards. It takes a team and not just individuals."

Matt continued talking about roles and teamwork. As someone that wanted to be a coach one day, he was passionate about these topics.

"It reminds me of a post I saw on social media that said 'Every team in America has five starters and a leading scorer. What does it matter if you are starting or a star player? Not every team in America wins. Winning is more difficult and special than being a starter or star'."

"Wow, that statement kind of punches you right between the eyes, huh?" Chaz said.

"That's probably the way those Patriot and Eagles teams went about their business," said Matt. "We before me. I'm guessing that's not just a cliché for those guys."

"The announcers also said that Julian Edelman was only like the 30th top receiver that year in the NFL, but he was the best for the Patriots. They didn't need individual star performances. They valued team performance, instead." Chaz pointed out.

"I like that the Eagles won a Super Bowl – with a backup quarterback, no less. Maybe there's hope for us Eagles, after all," said Antonio.

"Maybe we need to start approaching things like those Super Bowl Eagles and don't be concerned about who gets the credit or accolades," Matt suggested. "More to the point, we have to put our egos to the side and be more concerned about the team. We play a team sport, after all."

"Hey, sorry to interrupt," said Chaz. "But here's the highlight I was telling you guys about that happened while we were playing today. They're showing that player from State whose coach went off on him today on national TV."

One of the players asked Mr. Frank to turn up the sound so they could hear it better and the booming voice of the TV host echoed throughout the bus.

"Today's big win by State isn't what leads our broadcast tonight," said the studio host. "Instead of the game's outcome being the most talked-about story in college basketball today, it's something that happened during the game itself that has everyone's attention."

The announcer's words could be heard while the video showed exactly what happened during a tense timeout.

"Early in the second half, Tom Winston committed one of his game-high eight turnovers. At the next timeout, we can see Coach Henry giving Winston an earful. It appears that the coach has to be restrained by some of Winston's teammates. This exchange went viral on social media with various people weighing in on both sides. We'll now hear from both Coach Henry and from Tom Winston at the post-game press conference."

The players saw State's coach seated at a table with a microphone in front of him.

"Our players come here because they want to be coached and because they want to be part of something bigger than themselves," State's Coach Henry could be heard saying on TV. "Our players know that I love them and want the best for them. Sure, I get upset sometimes when our standards are not met, or players are not doing things in the best interest of the team. We don't have 12 players with their own individual agendas. We have 12 players that support, love, and encourage one another. They also want to make sure that they don't let each other down. Tom was not living up to the standards that he had set for himself. He was not focused, and he was not being a team player. I was not out of control, but he definitely needed to wake up and realize how his actions were affecting his team."

The TV coverage then switched to a different person sitting in the same room at the same table. State's Tom Winston was now addressing the media and his words could be heard clearly and there was no mistaking his thoughts on the matter.

"People just see Coach yelling at me and going all crazy. Coach is passionate. He doesn't do things quietly but what people don't see is the love he has for each of us," said State's Tom Winston. "I was letting my teammates down. It wasn't just about turning the ball over. It was how I turned the ball over. My man had just scored, and I was determined to get back at him, so I forced the action and tried to play my own game. My own game led me right into trouble and I lost the ball. Making matters worse, I loafed back on defense. I was doing my own thing and that's not how we do things here. That's how bad teams do things but not us. That doesn't fly here."

James and Antonio looked at each other in disbelief as the player from State continued with his surprising comments.

"I didn't even think it was a big deal at the time," Tom Winston said. "I've told Coach Henry a bunch of times that he can be hard on me. I've told him I want to be coachable and be the best that I can be. I was surprised when I looked at my phone just a few minutes ago and saw all the messages and all the stuff about this going viral. I needed to refocus during the game. I don't worry about how Coach says something to me. I just worry about what he's saying to me. I want to always be improving. I know that when Coach is yelling at me or getting after me, it's never out of harm. It's never out of hate. I interact with him every single day and we have a bond. A connection. I know that he pushes me because he wants the best for me. He's a great coach and an even better person. He is also an emotional person. I love Coach. I love my teammates. I'm glad that I get to be part of this program."

As the TV went to commercial, the bus was silent. It was safe to say that the players on the bus had not heard a player say those kinds of things before. But then again, most of them had not been around a program with as good of culture like the one at State.

"Wow! I guess that's all that I can say. Wow!" Chaz repeated.

"I can tell you right now I don't know if I would've defended Coach if he yelled at me like that," James admitted.

"It would be hard. But then again, State seems to have something special," Antonio pointed out. "That dude said he wanted to be coachable. He wanted to be coached hard. He wanted to improve. It makes me wonder about me."

"What about you? What do you mean?" asked James.

"Well, I know for a fact that I've gotten defensive in the past when coaches questioned whether or not I was coachable," admitted Antonio. "I've always thought I was coachable."

"We probably all think that we're coachable. But maybe our coaches or teammates don't see us that way," Chaz acknowledged.

Antonio was serious about this and wanted everyone sitting around him to know it.

"I want to be the best player I can be," Antonio said in Matt's direction since he knew that Matt was always a team-oriented guy.

"I don't doubt that but are you wanting to be good for you or for the team?" Matt asked him.

Antonio thought about that question for a moment and then responded, "Winston said a bunch of interesting things just now, but there was something that bothered me because I've said it a bunch. He mentioned 'playing his game'."

"Yeah, so has your mom," James said. "I've heard her lots of times. 'Just play your game, baby. Just play your game. You do you'. I can hear her now."

"Like your mom hasn't probably yelled something like that out during a game, either." Mentioned Chaz as he came to Antonio's defense.

"Touché," James responded.

It was obvious that Antonio was serious about his thoughts right now because he didn't bite or get caught up in his roommate's jokes.

"Tom Winston was trying to do his own thing and it hurt his team," Antonio acknowledged. "Maybe when I'm trying to improve, it's essentially so I can look better personally. My motive might not be to improve so the team is better but so I get more exposure or attention."

"That makes sense. I don't know. You might be on to something," said Chaz.

"If I'm serious about wanting to be coachable then I should probably start to look at myself honestly and whether or not I'm in it for myself or the team," Antonio said.

Matt shook his head in agreement. He was liking how Antonio was starting to question some of these things. Matt was going to try to keep the momentum going as long as Antonio was willing to considering all of this team stuff.

Matt said, "I like those thoughts, Antonio. Just like those Super Bowl Eagles. 'We before me'. Maybe us Eagles can become like that. Remember in Dr. Forest's business class when he had us watch those *Shark Tank* episodes?"

"Some of them were pretty cool. I'd be trying to get Mark Cuban and Daymond John to go in together and be my partner every time. Those dudes are awesome!" said Antonio.

"Yeah! Remember when he showed us the one about the lady that put mirrors in dressing rooms so when people tried on clothes, they looked skinnier and then bought the clothes because they liked the way they looked?" asked Matt.

"That was funny," Chaz said as he recalled watching that episode in Dr. Forest's class. "The reflection people saw wasn't real or accurate. But they definitely liked what they saw. I remember that one. It was kind of dishonest and she didn't get a deal if I remember. Why do you bring that up?"

Matt answered, "As we were talking about being coachable and being team players, I was thinking that none of us thinks we're selfish or that we're uncoachable as Antonio mentioned a few minutes ago. Maybe we're looking at ourselves like people looking at one of those weird mirrors. Maybe we're not honestly assessing ourselves."

"You may be on to something there," Antonio said acknowledging Matt's observation.

"You guys know that I love Steph Curry," Matt reminded them. "Well, he stayed an extra year in school when people were saying he should leave for the NBA. Even though he was a great shooter and scorer, he stayed that extra year so that he could play the point guard position for the entire year. That allowed him to become an even better player."

Steph Curry had nearly doubled his assist average from his sophomore to his junior year, remarkably without sacrificing his scoring average.

Matt thought of another example and said, "How about Michael Jordan? James, you'll like this. MJ, as you probably know to be as big of a fan as you are, couldn't shoot a lick when he first came into the league. But after five years in the league, he finally got serious about his overall game and worked on his three-point shooting. Low and behold, the Bulls finally got over the hump and started winning championships after that. I don't think that was merely a coincidence.

"And don't forget about Kevin Durant," Chaz added.

"I know what you're going to say." Interrupted Antonio. "Coach loves mentioning that quote from one of KD's former coaches. It's even on a poster in his office."

"Kevin Durant works like he's trying to make the team." quoted James.

"We make fun of Coach for mentioning quote a lot, but it's kind of a cool statement. It'd be awesome if a coach said that about me. It's one thing if I was terrible and was actually just trying to make the team. But when you're a star like KD, that's a pretty cool compliment. Outworking your talent. That's a phrase Coach likes to say," Chaz said.

As a future coach, Matt loved the direction that this conversation had gone. Because these teammates were friends and shared a mutual love of sports, they were able to banter back and forth but also learn some lessons.

Matt added, "Kawhi Leonard was just like MJ. He couldn't shoot coming out of college but then worked on his shooting and become one of the best players in the NBA."

"And he has some rings to show for that," Antonio pointed out as he rubbed his fingers wishing they were home to some of that bling.

"You're right," Matt agreed. "He and his teammates have rings to show for his coachability and improvement."

"I'm starting to think that all this coachability and improvement stuff might actually be important," joked Chaz. "If I can make myself better, then maybe I can help this Eagles team be like the Super Bowl Eagles team."

Matt agreed with Chaz, "I think you're right. Instead of getting defensive or being overly sensitive to what Coach has to say to us in practice or meetings, we should take it as an opportunity to get better."

"Just like State's Tom Winston," Antonio added.

"Exactly," said Matt. "We all want to be part of a great team, but a great team requires great teammates. Are we those people on this team? I guess if we aren't coachable then we won't have a championship team like State," Matt suggested.

"Or the Super Bowl Eagles," added Antonio.

"Yes, our beloved namesake." Said Chaz.

DREAM TEAM

The football game had finished but the Eagles still had some time left on their trip. For those not sleeping, Satellite TV still offered many entertainment options.

"Hey Coach, please keep it on this channel," James asked. "Michael Jordan's my favorite and that documentary about the Dream Team is coming up next."

"I heard Charles Barkley was also on that team," said Antonio. "I'm guessing he was probably a lot skinnier, then."

"He was," said Coach Dunn. "They called him the 'Round Mound of Rebound' because he was a little bit pudgy when he played. I will tell you though, he was extremely athletic. Barkley was a complete player. He was a competitor. He was an all-time great player, just like most of the guys on the Dream Team."

"They went undefeated in the 1992 Olympics, right?" asked James.

"Not only did they go undefeated, but they won all of their games by an average margin of 44 points!" Coach Dunn said.

Antonio turned to his roommate as the documentary's opening credits were playing and it went to commercial, "Hey James, how come you're such a big Michael Jordan fan? Didn't he retire way before we were even born?"

"Pretty much, but my dad was the been the biggest MJ fan ever," James said. "While growing up, I only had three posters on my walls."

"Oh, wait, let me guess," interrupted Antonio excitedly. "Jonas Brothers, Thomas the Train, and, of course, Beyoncé."

"Um, no. Not quite, funny guy," responded James shaking his head at how silly his roommate was. "My dad let me have a poster of the Rock and Ice Cube."

"And let me guess," interrupted Antonio again. "The third one was drum roll, please. Michael Jordan!"

"Exactly. But it wasn't one of those with MJ dunking or doing his Air Jordan thing. It was this poster of just him with his six championship rings. My dad always said it was his favorite because it was about championships and not individual accomplishments."

"Hmmm," said Chaz.

"What do you mean 'hmmm'. What's that for?" asked James a little bit defensively.

"Nothing don't worry about it," Chaz said.

"You must have meant something by it."

"Nah, just messing with you," Chaz responded. "The commercials are over. Time to get back to watching more of this old-fashioned history channel stuff."

"They are kind of old, aren't they. And the shorts. OMG! Coach, did you play in those kinds of shorts?" asked James.

"Hey Coach," Antonio called out. "Can you turn up the volume. James is talking way too much back here!"

At the next commercial break, Antonio, Chaz, and James continued their conversation.

"Did you catch what they said?" asked Antonio. "The Dream Team only had one team rule? We have five million rules. I hope Coach heard about only having one rule."

"But if we only had the one rule that the Dream Team had, you and James would be toast," Chaz pointed out.

"I meant that I wish Coach only had one rule," Antonio corrected what he'd said. "I didn't necessarily mean I want that one rule to be the Dream Team's rule."

"Hypothetically, what if our only rule was the Dream Team's only rule?" Chaz asked. "What if our only rule was 'Be on Time'? How would you handle that?"

"I don't know. That'd be scary," James admitted. "But it'd be good for you since you're never late."

"I guess you're right. I wouldn't have to worry about it, personally, but we'd probably be missing you guys for most of our games," Chaz said looking at both James and Antonio with a huge grin on his face.

"Come to think of it," said Chaz as he reconsidered. "I guess it'd actually be good for me, personally. I'd get to play more. Yes, the more I think about it, the more I think that should be our only rule. All-Conference, here I come!"

"I don't know if he's being serious or not, but Chaz does make a decent point," admitted Antonio. "We're always late and that probably isn't fair to the rest of the team."

"You're right Antonio," said James. "It's never been anything I've thought about, but it was important enough of a rule to be the only rule on the Dream Team. Their coach said they did it because it was more than just about being late for a bus or team meal. It was about respect. It was a sign that the person didn't think they were better than somebody else. I never thought about it that way."

Chaz mentioned, "Like this morning when you guys stopped to get food and were late getting on the bus."

"I was hungry," justified Antonio. "And it was a really good biscuit, you know."

"You're not kidding," echoed James. "Those tasted so good it makes you wanna slap yo mama!"

"That's right!" said Antonio.

"Slap yo mama? I don't even know what you're talking about right now," Chaz said shaking his head.

91

"It's from *Friday After Next*. You know, with Ice Cube?" said James. "Forget about it. It doesn't matter. Anyway, those biscuits were ridiculously good, but I think I get your point. We made the whole team late. At the very least we weren't very respectful of your guys' time."

"But those biscuits were good," Antonio pointed out again.

"Mmm, mmm, mmm," James said as his mouth was nearly watering just thinking about them.

Chaz was starting to get a little frustrated, but it might have been because he was jealous that he didn't get one of those biscuits this morning.

"Okay, got it. The biscuits were good. They were probably better than what I ate, but James, what did you think about your guy, MJ?" Chaz asked.

"First of all, I was surprised that they even had rules at all for a team that good," said James. "Only having one rule was also very interesting. I would have thought it'd be no profanity or fighting or complaining or talking back to a coach. You know, something like that. But you mention my guy MJ. It was awesome how the next day after that rules meeting, he was the first guy on the bus, and he was there 30 minutes early."

"I think they said the latest any Dream Team player ever was for the bus or a meeting was ten minutes EARLY," said a clearly impressed Antonio. "How is that even possible?"

"Well, they were not just the most talented players in the world, but they were also the best players in the world. They were the best for a reason. There were lots of talented players that didn't make that team. These guys were the best of the best," Chaz reminded them.

"Make sense," acknowledged James. "It's funny how competitive MJ was that he even wanted to be the first on the bus."

Chaz had an idea and he couldn't help but get a sly smile across his face.

"Hey James, how about next game, you and Antonio battle each other out and see who is more competitive. See which of you can win that contest. See which of you can get here first."

"That might be tough, especially if those biscuits just calling my name, 'James, baby. 'James, honey. James, my dear'. Now be quiet, the commercial's over and I want to see that clip that Coach was talking about where Charles Barkley elbowed that opposing player and about broke him in half because Barkley was so strong."

"Oh boy," said Chaz rolling his eyes. "That's a whole different thing to talk about one day. The Barkley elbow, slappin' yo mama. Sheesh!"

BACK AT SCHOOL

The bus started to slow down and Learie looked out the window and saw the sign for their exit.

"That's a sight for sore eyes," said Learie.

"Almost there. Can't wait for my head to hit that bed," said Brandon.

"No kidding," Learie said. "I only have one class tomorrow. I'm not going to lie. I'm pretty tired. I'm not entirely disappointed we don't have practice tomorrow."

"I agree. It was pretty obvious that Coach didn't really want to see us much tomorrow," Brandon stated.

"He was a little frustrated with us, wasn't he?"

Learie then continued with a thought, "I've been thinking about something ever since we talked earlier."

"What's that?" Brandon asked.

"I think what you and I talked about would be good for everyone to hear," suggested Learie. "Even though we aren't having practice, I think we should get everyone together tomorrow."

"A team meeting?" Brandon asked.

"A team meeting," Learie said. "But not one of those players-only ones where everyone moans and complains. What we talked about is pretty important. It could spur something on in other people's minds, as well. I mean, if it got me thinking, maybe it will get others thinking."

Brandon agreed, "That's a good idea. I'll text everyone right now."

All across the bus, the sound of dings and beeps could be heard as Brandon's text message was delivered to his teammate's phones.

"That's weird," mentioned Brandon looking at his phone.

"What's that?"

"Everyone responded," said Brandon.

"Even James and Antonio?" asked Learie.

"Yes, even the dynamic duo. But that isn't what's weird," said Brandon. "Not only did everyone respond but nobody complained even though we're supposed to have the day off. That's the unusual part."

"Cool. Guess I can't take as long of an afternoon nap tomorrow as I was hoping," Learie said.

"Nope, but I think your idea of a meeting will be a good thing. In the long run, I think it will be better than your nap."

The players felt the bus come to a stop in the parking lot outside the gymnasium.

"Rise and shine fellas. Your chariot has arrived back at the castle," announced Mr. Frank.

"Your what and where?" said Learie.

"That's just Mr. Frank," Brandon said. "I'm not really sure what he's saying sometimes but I guess I know what he means."

"Whatever. I'm just glad to be home. Let's get off this bus."

As the players cleaned up around their seats, picked up the trash, and gathered their things, Jaylen approached Coach Dunn with a limp as he navigated the bus aisle with his crutches.

"Hey, Coach. I know that today was rough," Jaylen said. "In fact, the whole season's been rough. But try and get some sleep tonight. I know that you're going to want to be up before the roosters tomorrow but try and sleep in a little later than usual. You're no good to us if you're tired and worn down. Even though you canceled practice because you were frustrated with us, we can turn that into a positive. Some of us can use the time to get into the training room extra or rest up. The same goes for you. Rest up a little. Use tomorrow to get a little refreshed and let's get back at it the day after."

"I appreciate that," Coach Dunn said. "I'll see what I can do."

"Also, just to keep you in the loop. We're having a team meeting tomorrow. It's supposed to be a good team meeting. I'll personally make sure that we stay focused on the positive stuff. I know that you've put a lot of trust in me over the years. I appreciate that. Trust me on this also, Coach."

"Thanks for letting me know."

Jaylen wanted to make sure that Coach wasn't worried about tomorrow's meeting so he said, "I know player-only meetings are often not very productive, but I was talking with Brandon and he assured me that this will be a positive thing and not like those meetings we hear about when a team rebels against a coach."

"Okay, thanks again, Jaylen. Have a good night."

Jaylen left the bus with Scott right behind him. Scott was another freshman on the team. He roomed with Travis. The two of them respected Jaylen a great deal. Scott and Jaylen had a class together right before lunch and often got a bite to eat together.

"Hey Jaylen, I just heard you talking with Coach about the meeting tomorrow. You also told him to get some rest and all that other stuff. That was different since you're a player and he's the Coach. I don't know if I've noticed that before. It was almost like you were coaching him."

"Not coaching. Just encouraging," Jaylen replied. "I know early on in my basketball career; I'd get mad when the coaches, teachers or even my parents wouldn't encourage me or praise me. About midway through my freshman year, I decided that instead of getting frustrated when somebody didn't acknowledge me or recognize me for something, I was going to turn that around and flip the script. I decided I would encourage or praise somebody, instead."

"You always seem like you've got an encouraging word for somebody when they are down. I can't imagine you not being an encourager."

"It's not that I wasn't encouraging people at all. I just wasn't doing it enough. I also found that I wasn't doing it when I was feeling down or frustrated, myself."

"You said it was your freshman year when this changed. Did you have some vision or something?" Scott asked with a smirk on his face.

"No vision or alien abduction. It was Psych class," Jaylen said. "The teacher was sharing about this guy, Karl Menninger, that had been on the cover of TIME Magazine and stuff like that. One day he was speaking to a large college class and somebody asked him what a person should do if they were depressed or distraught. The person asking the question assumed that this noted psychologist would mention some kind of counseling or cutting-edge treatment. Instead, Menninger said 'board up the house, go across the street, find someone in need, and go help them'. When I heard that I decided to start encouraging others more. The only way for me to beat despair or frustrations was through engagement. I had to get out of my own little world. I had to stop being selfish and encourage others. If I felt like I wasn't getting the encouragement, recognition, or praise that I wanted, then I was going to make sure that somebody else didn't feel that way, either."

"I never thought about it quite like that before."

"I hadn't either," Jaylen said. "I also realized that it's not just my teammates that need encouraging. But my teachers, parents, custodians, coaches, even Mr. Frank. All of those people need a kind word, smile, or breath of fresh air blown into their lives once in a while."

"You might want to consider starting your own greeting card company," Scott suggested. "You've got some great insights and deep thoughts."

"Thanks for the encouragement, Scott. I appreciate it. You asked me about Coach to start with and I wanted you to know that I'm not trying to kiss up to him. That's not my intention. I just try to encourage him whenever I can. And it's not hollow encouragement. It's not the fake stuff. It's not like, 'hey Coach, we all love you so keep doing what you're doing'. That wouldn't really benefit anyone."

Scott chuckled and nodded his head in agreement. "I hate it when people are like 'you can do it' or 'let's go' but they are being very generic. That doesn't motivate me very much."

"You're right. We should be saying things that have substance," Jaylen said. "We can always find something to encourage someone with. Even if one of my teammates is playing poorly, I can remind them of when they performed great. I can speak to the value they can bring to the team."

As he heard Jaylen say that, Scott's eyes got real big as he remembered a situation during the previous week.

"Now that you say that, I remember last week when you said 'Scott, you can do this. You can get a stop just like in the game against Tech when you slapped the floor, got in that stance, and forced their guard to go left, totally disrupting that key play'. That motivated me because you put something real in my head. You didn't just say 'you can do it; you can do it' while clapping a lot."

Jaylen smiled at Scott's comment, "That's what I mean. We can always find some way to encourage others. I know that I love it when others compliment me or encourage me, so it has to work the same with others. If I can encourage others, then they might be a little more motivated. If we're all doing that, then before you know it, maybe we have a team that's totally looking out for each other and lifting each other up. That goes for all of us, coaches, managers, support staff, and players. We're all in this together."

"Never thought of that," Scott said. "Thanks for sharing. See you tomorrow."

TEAM MEETING

A s the players trickled in, there was something different about the atmosphere. It wasn't depressing like the room normally was after a loss.

James and Antonio were also two of the first people there. That was remarkably strange but in a good way.

"Hey, James. Hey, Antonio. Sorry about the mix up in time," said Brandon.

"What do you mean?" asked James.

"Well, you're here early. It's not yet 4:00. You must have thought I said 3:30 or something like that."

"Haha funny, Brandon," said Antonio. "We heard the right time. We're just here early."

"Cool. I'm just messing with you. We'll get started soon,"

"That's fine. We were just a little convicted watching that documentary last night about the Dream Team," said James. "If it was good enough for the best team ever in the history of sports, then maybe we should be a little bit more respectful and start being on time."

"Plus, maybe one day Mr. Frank will be sick, and we'll have a substitute bus driver that actually leaves us behind," added Antonio with a smile.

"I'm not sure a bus driver would leave a player behind but maybe Coach would finally follow through on his threats," said Brandon.

Almost in unison, James and Antonio repeated the line that Coach Dunn had often said, "My Coach left me behind my senior year of college and so any of you could get left behind also."

"Regardless though," said Brandon. "You guys are saying things that are directly related to why Learie and I wanted to have a team meeting today."

By now, all 12 players had arrived, so Learie opened up the meeting.

"Brandon and I were talking last night on the bus. I'm sure that you all heard that my dad got on Coach pretty hard after the game. That is how the conversation with Brandon started. We've been friends for a long time so he could say some things to me that if someone else said them, I'm not sure I would have listened."

Learie continued, "During our talk, I came to realize that I wasn't taking responsibility for my actions. I was making way too many excuses. Because I'm a senior, I've been getting more and more frustrated about not playing. But this was leading me to act less and less as a senior should act. I realized that I was not being the leader that this team needed whether I was playing or not. I wasn't setting a good example. I wasn't taking responsibility for my actions."

"Learie is right," said Brandon. "Our night started off rocky with the poor performance in the game and then his dad got up in Coach's grill. But I think some good came out of it. We might meet with the officials before each game. We might have a 'C' next to our name on the roster. Our resume might say 'Captain'. All those things might be true, but we have to be more positive leaders.

"Sure, Learie has made excuses and not always acted like a captain but we can all do better," continue Brandon. "We can all take more responsibility for our actions. After all, we have a collective responsibility. We're responsible to and for each other. Our actions and attitudes affect more than just us. Overall, as your leaders, we haven't done what we need to do. We have a position, and maybe some status, but we haven't earned it day after day. We need to do a better job of helping this team be the best it can be. Not everything that happens is our fault just because we're captains, but it is our responsibility to find a way to make things better. We're the team captains and we need to do everything we can to make sure that we're getting better and creating the right culture. You guys need us to be better leaders. We may be your captains. We may have a position of leadership, but you need us to actually be good leaders."

The room was silent. Every eye was focused on Brandon and Learie as they spoke. What they were saying was a surprise, but it made sense in a weird way that the players had not previously thought about. As they processed their words, they realized that Learie and Brandon may be right, but the team had confidence they would be the leaders they needed moving forward.

"Hey guys, thanks for sharing," said Jaylen. "I don't know about the rest of the team, but I believe in you and am glad that you are our captains. You guys are leaders, but it makes sense what you are saying. There's always room for improvement. Plus, we probably haven't been very good followers, either. We can all do better."

"I agree with Jaylen," said Matt. "You guys are our captains for a reason. Whether or not you think you've done a good job, doesn't matter right now. All that matters now is that you want to get better and that motivates me. I want to get better, too. If you think you can do better, then we all should feel the same way and want to make ourselves better."

Matt continued with his thought, "What you're saying is interesting, because Chaz and I had a conversation last night, too. We talked about starring in your role. About excelling in a role. When you are excellent in the role you have, everybody on the team benefits. Championship teams are made up of a bunch of stars. Not necessarily people in the spotlight but people excelling in their roles that complement one another. There were some things I hadn't really thought much about before. Talking with Chaz last night and then hearing you today makes me really want to try to be better and make this team better moving forward."

"Well aren't you all just so precious," said James sarcastically. "Here Antonio and I thought we were the ones trying to turn over a new leaf, start fresh, and begin living right. But, nooooo! You guys have to go and steal our thunder. We thought we'd be the ones looking good since we were late but with this confessional taking place, I just don't know. Seriously though, this is awesome. By the way, in case you didn't notice or hear me the first time, Antonio and I were on time today."

"Actually, you were early," said Learie with a smirk.

"Okay, yeah, but I didn't want to go full on brag-mode," said James. "Anyway, we were early to this meeting because we realized last night that by being late to everything, we were essentially disrespecting all of you. We were saying that we were more important than you guys. We were acting all entitled and everything. We're sorry and will try to do better in the future. No guarantees that we'll always be early like today, but we should always be on time from here on out."

"James is definitely speaking for me about all of this stuff," echoed Antonio. "But listening to him talk, along with what Matt said and Brandon and Learie said, I think this meeting went a different direction than most of us probably expected after a loss."

Just as remarkably as James and Antonio showing up early to a meeting, 12 heads seemed to be simultaneously shaking up and down in unanimous agreement.

WHITEBOARD

The meeting had started in a surprising way and the co-captains were determined to take advantage of the positive vibe they were getting from the rest of their team.

"Wow, I didn't expect this when we called this meeting," said Learie. "I really just wanted to apologize for being a bad leader and making excuses all the time. Brandon and I were wanting to let you know that we were going to do better, but it sounds like some of you also had productive conversations last night. If you guys don't mind, let's take a few more minutes and talk about these things. We can even act like Coach and write some stuff on the white board so we can visualize it a little better."

Brandon took his cue from Learie, picked up the dry erase marker, and approached the white board.

"Like Learie and I said, we want to be more than captains. We want to be positive leaders. As we talked about, we need to take more responsibility. Specifically, we need to stop making excuses. We could all stand to do better in this area at times, so I'm going to write down 'Lose the excuses'."

After writing down 'Lose the excuses', Brandon continued. "Matt and Chaz, you guys talked about starring and excelling in your roles.

What if I put 'Excel in your role', does that sum up your conversation last night?'"

"Yeah, that works," said Matt.

"And our dynamic duo of promptness and punctuality have finally seen the light and admitted that our time matters as well," joked Brandon.

"Why don't you just write down 'Always be on time' and stop busting our chops," suggested Antonio.

"Deal," said Brandon. "So, we wrote three things up here. Anyone have anything to add?"

"Well, as long as it's confessional time," joked Drew. "I'd like to point out that our fearless leader up there with the dry erase marker made me feel guilty when we were stopped in traffic forever after the game."

"It was only like 15 minutes and if you felt guilty, it's because you had a guilty conscience already as opposed to it being something I said," replied Brandon.

"Anyway, for those of you that didn't hear," continued Drew. "He said that my attitude was like a flat tire and I wouldn't get very far if I didn't fix it. I realized that I haven't been displaying the best attitude. I guess I can be grumpy and that doesn't spread enthusiasm or positivity. In fact, it can be quite contagious, like a sickness or something."

"Yeah, we don't want you to be a germ," said Brandon.

"He's right," added Jaylen. "We want you to be a big dose of Vitamin-C, or D, or E, or whatever that thing is in orange juice that's supposed to make us healthy."

"Anyway. No, I don't want to be a germ. I need to do a better job displaying a good attitude," agreed Brandon.

"I think that's something we all should be doing so I'm going to add 'Display a good attitude' to the board. Thanks for sharing," said Brandon.

After writing on the board, Brandon looked at Scott, who was raising his hand, and smiled.

"Hey Scott. you don't have to raise your hand to speak. This isn't class or anything like that. If you have something to say, be sure to speak up and just say it."

"Sorry. Habit," said the freshman. "Anyway, I'm sure you've noticed but Jaylen always has a really good attitude. He's always encouraging people."

The teammates nodded their heads in approval.

"Yeah, you probably knew that. But what you may not have seen him do which I was able to witness is how he encouraged Coach last night. Come to find out he does that frequently. I know he has encouraged me throughout the year. By the looks on your faces, I know you agree with me. But it goes further. He encourages more than just his fellow teammates. He encourages everyone," said Scott.

"You're right Scott," said Brandon. "Jaylen is quick with a compliment or praise. He always tries to be positive. He has encouraged me a bunch through the years. It's no surprise he encourages everybody in our program, not just his teammates. We're all a family. We're one program. I'm actually going to put what you said on the board."

Brandon then wrote 'Encourage team members' on the white board.

"I put team members instead of teammates because we should also strive to encourage managers, trainers, bus drivers, coaches, whoever. We're all in this together."

"Hey Brandon."

Brandon looked at Antonio half expecting him to pat himself on the back again for being on time, but that wasn't why Antonio was speaking up.

"Mr. Frank's story about that gold guy, R.U. Darby, really spoke to me. I also liked hearing about that explorer guy."

"Cortez," interrupted Bobbi who was trying to help out Antonio.

"Yeah, thanks, Mr. Book Worm," responded Antonio. "Anyway, I realized I probably wasn't very committed to this team or the process or the journey if I was getting frustrated too easily and always losing focus. It's been about me way too much, especially when I'm not scoring many points, like last night. When this happens and I'm not committed to the team, then I'm probably not much good to anyone. I don't think I have been committed to the team or focused very well lately and that is something that I'm going to work on."

"Along with being on time," James reminded him.

"Great point, both of you," said Brandon. "Antonio, I agree with what you are saying but it isn't just you. I hadn't heard of either of those stories before Mr. Frank and Coach told them to us. But they spoke to me, too. We thought we would be good this year and for a bunch of different reasons we have underachieved. But maybe if we remain committed to the process and focused on our goal, then we might be close to that mother lode like R.U. Darby. I think this applies to all of us, so I'm going to write down 'Remain committed and focused'."

"We had a bunch of players-only meetings at my high school," said Matt. "But none of them were like this."

"I can't say that I've been in one like this either," Drew concurred. "They're normally gripe sessions. Come to think of it, I probably did most of the complaining. But so far, I've really liked the way this has been going."

There was a slight pause in the conversation and so Travis took the opportunity to share what was on his mind.

"Scott already mentioned how Jaylen is such an encourager, but I want to say something else about him that I think can apply to all of us. Well, I was talking with Jaylen in the training room yesterday after he hurt his knee. We all know that he's a ball of energy and one of the hardest workers we've ever seen but I realized those qualities don't need to be limited to just him. We can have 12 guys doing the same thing. It doesn't matter our talent level or status. I decided that I'm going to try and be like Jaylen. I want to put forth as much effort as possible. I want to supply this team with energy. I'm just warning you guys that I'm coming at you in practice and you better rise up if you want to win any sprints from now. I'm bringing it."

"That's awesome. I love it," said Brandon. "I think you're right. It stinks that Jaylen is going to be out of commission, but we can all pick up the slack. We can all do this."

And then Brandon wrote the phrase 'Supply effort and energy' on the board.

Drew then spoke up again, "Brandon, I know I already mentioned about my attitude in the traffic jam, but I wanted to bring up something else that I learned last night. For those of you who don't know, I was served a dessert called humble pie yesterday when we stopped to eat. I thought I was right, but I was dead wrong. I saw a great example of servant leadership from the restaurant manager. It was not normal, or at least my normal. I realized how selfish I can be and how I can get so obsessed with seeing just my tree and not the whole forest. I can get consumed with only my stuff. But to have a great team, we need each other. We need to help each other. We need to serve each other. This is not a concept that will be easy for me, but I realize I need to try and do better in this area."

Brandon had a big smile on his face as he listened to Drew speak. He was remembering the scene last night from the restaurant.

"I was watching that whole thing from the other table and thought it was funny," said Brandon. "Especially Bobbi getting all red in the face and sweating because he ate a spicy chicken. Glad that you weren't allergic or anything, Bobbi.

"Me too," said Bobbi.

"Drew, thanks for sharing," said Brandon. "That's going to be a tough one for many of us but we probably all need to think of each other a little bit more. We need to think about what's best for each other. This could be a key lesson as we look to finish the year strong, so I'm going to list it with the others that we've written down."

'Help and serve others' was then written on the board.

James then posed a question to his teammates, "I don't know how many of you have ever been dog-cussed out by a coach."

"Does a parent count?" asked Demetrius.

"Sure does. I'm really just asking if it's happened to you. Doesn't really matter who did it," continued James. "I've been taken to the woodshed many times by my AAU and high school coaches. I've probably deserved it every time even though I probably didn't act like I deserved it. I'm sure every single time this happened I passed the buck or didn't take responsibility, like the first thing you wrote down.

"Hey, lose those excuses!" joked his roommate Antonio.

"I know. That's what I'm saying," continued James. "I'm sure I made excuses and they were probably good ones at the time, so what you guys listed as the first principle is very relevant to me. But when I saw that dude from State get ripped last night on TV and then respond the way he did, it set something off in me. I mean in a good way, not the normal way of setting something off. It was like a slap in the face. It was a wakeup call. I realized that I've never responded that way even when it was my fault. Dude said it was his fault and he wanted to improve. I've had coaches tell me that I'm uncoachable and I normally blow it off or get defensive. That dude from State was coachable. He certainly didn't respond like have done in the past. I need whatever it is he's having. I need to be more like that. If you guys have any suggestions, please let me know but I just thought I'd mention it."

Brandon asked James, "Would it be okay if I wrote it on the board. I think that's a principle that is important and can apply to all of us."

"Sure, man. It seems good. However you want to sum up what I just said is fine with me," said James.

"Thanks for sharing. I'm going to put 'Improve and be coachable' because none of us know everything and we can always get better and the way most of us can get better is to be coachable."

"Sounds good to me," said James.

Brandon looked at his watch, put down the marker, and then turned to his teammates.

"We've been here long enough, and I appreciate all of the honesty and things you guys have said. This has certainly been one of the most productive meetings I've been a part of. I really wasn't prepared for this. Like I said, Learie and I just wanted to share our thoughts on excuses and taking responsibility for our actions. I wasn't ready for all of you to share like you did but it was awesome."

"Hey Brandon," said Demetrius. "I'm sorry to interrupt you but you mentioned that you weren't prepared for what was going to be said at this meeting. That must have been a sign that you used that word. I wasn't going to say anything because we've been here long enough, but you said that word and I think it's important."

"I agree but why do you say it's important. What are you thinking?" asked Brandon.

"The word 'prepared' stood out to me because I wasn't prepared for the game yesterday. In fact, I'm rarely prepared because I don't play much. Bobbi and I were talking and he kind of lit into me about how my being unprepared can actually lead to me losing out on opportunities. It can also hurt the team and you guys are my friends. Champions are prepared. Winners are prepared. I know some of us have not been taking things as seriously as we can. We haven't prepared as well as we can. I'm certainly at the top of that list, but I don't think it's a coincidence that we're playing badly and having a poor season. Whether it's practice, weights, sleep, scouting reports, or anything else, we need to do better if we want to win."

Since Bobbi was involved in that conversation, he felt the urge to support his teammate in what he was saying.

"Demetrius is right. We may have some tight games moving forward and our preparation might just be the difference between winning and losing. I think Demetrius can be valuable to us moving forward if he is prepared. In fact, we can all be valuable to each other by being more prepared," said Bobbi.

"My grandma has this little magnet thing on her refrigerator," Brandon said. "It's some old guy from medieval times or something. His name is Sun Tzu but evidently, he said that 'the battle is won or lost before it is fought'. Maybe if we all prepare a little harder then we might win a little bit more. That was a good one. So, thanks, Demetrius."

'Prepare to win' then became the tenth principle that Brandon wrote on the white board. It was hard to believe that in one day, in one bus trip, a team could learn so many crucial lessons.

LEADERSHIP

The meeting appeared over and a lot of great things had been discussed. The team was feeling good about themselves when Bobbi spoke up.

"Uhmmm, has anyone else noticed something about what we wrote down?"

Twelve sets of eyeballs looked at the white board and the ten principles that were listed. They were trying to figure out what Bobbi had noticed.

It seemed like forever but was just over a minute when Jaylen became the first to speak.

"I love puzzles and I'm seeing that white board like one of those word puzzles I used to do on the back of those menus they'd have at restaurants for us kids. I'm seeing the word LEADERSHIP on that board."

"I see it now too," said Travis. "Wow, that's freaky. Is that what you saw Bobbi?"

"Sure is. That's some freaky stuff but also kind of cool," said Bobbi. "How's that for coincidences? It's almost like we were supposed to learn those lessons and write them down. Wow, how weird is that?"

Even though Bobbi was the first to see the hidden word on the whiteboard, now every set of eyes saw it as clear as day. It was like they had just solved a hidden message with their super-secret decoder ring.

Lose the excuses

Excel in your role

Always be on time

Display a good attitude

Encourage team members

Remain committed & focused

Supply effort & energy

Help & serve others

Improve & be coachable

Prepare to win

"Regardless of how weird it is, that's a good lesson for us," said Matt. "Each of these things can apply to all of us. None of us are immune to any of those things. They all apply at some point. Also, each of us can do each one of those things. It's not like Brandon is the only one that can improve and be coachable or that Learie is expected to be the only one who has to lose the excuses. Regardless of our status on the team, we can all do these things."

"That's right. We can all be leaders," added Jaylen. "If we do those things then we're demonstrating positive leadership. This will help the entire team. It's like leadership is the glue for all of these principles. Even though Brandon and Learie are our senior captains, we can all do these things. We can all practice and demonstrate leadership by doing these ten things."

"Since this is obviously like a big neon sign flashing at us saying be better and do better, what is our next step? How do we do these things now?" asked Bobbi.

"First, we definitely need to take a picture of this," said Brandon.

"Already did," Jaylen quickly replied.

"In that case. Maybe we make a poster or something like that," suggested Learie.

"I think that's a great idea, but I feel like we should do more," said Matt. "We already have some cool posters in our locker room, but we haven't really been living up to those. I don't want this to end up the same."

"I don't think it would end up being ignored, so to speak, because we actually came up with this stuff, not Coach," suggested Brandon. "Don't get me wrong. The posters he put up are pretty cool and say great things, but at the end of the day, they're his. However we did it, we actually came up with these things on our own. We can take ownership in this acronym thing. Sure, it should be a poster, but we need to be reminded of this often and live it out daily somehow."

"I agree. Last night's revelations and these things we came up with are too special to just dismiss. This needs to be special somehow," said Jaylen.

"You mean like a blood oath?" joked Antonio.

"We don't need to light candles or get out the knives," responded Brandon. "Nothing creepy like that."

"How about we all sign the board like a contract, or an agreement or something like that," suggested Bobbi.

Learie wasted no time, picked up two dry erase markers, and tossed them to Antonio and James.

"You guys were the first ones here today. Go ahead and be the first to sign the board"

Antonio and James must have liked Bobbi's idea because they didn't hesitate to get up from their seats and sign the board.

Each of the remaining ten players then took their turns signing the board in an unofficial covenant to what their standards would be for the remainder of the season.

Jaylen announced to his teammates, "I just took another picture of the board. I wanted to get one with all of the signatures on it."

"Good idea," said Brandon. "Send that to me and I'll ask Coach to make it into a poster that goes right next to the door as we leave the locker room. That way we'll see it every time we leave."

As he finished talking, Brandon couldn't help but smile as he saw Scott raise his hand again.

"I thought I said there's no need to raise your hand."

"Uh, yeah. Sorry. Anyway, I was thinking that your poster idea is cool. But we should also get something we can all have. Like mini posters in our lockers or t-shirts or wristbands or something like that."

"I agree. Those are all great ideas," said Learie. "I actually like the wristband idea the best. Maybe get the word LEADERSHIP on them in our school colors."

"And Coach might even let us wear them in practice." added Bobbi. "That way we'd constantly be reminding ourselves and each other."

"Great ideas, guys," said Brandon. "I'll ask him about both the wristbands and the poster."

RIVALRY GAME

Normally practice the day before a game was more laid back and consisted of a lot of fine-tuning. This was not a normal practice the day before a game.

The players were more vocal than usual. Every loose ball was a battle. The energy was high.

Jaylen, who had in fact torn his ACL, gave his Coach a summary of yesterday's meeting. Coach Dunn believed what was discussed was genuine he hadn't expected the principles to take hold this quickly.

"Great practice, today! That's the way to bounce back from your last game."

Even though all the players were thinking it, Learie was the one that spoke first.

"We've dug ourselves quite a hole, but we're determined to finish the season strong. We know how we need to go about our business, Coach. We're sorry for how we've been handling ourselves this year and that changes now."

"I appreciate that. I believe you guys."

In all his years of coaching, Denny Dunn had thought he'd seen it all. But the way this team approached today's practice. The way all 12 guys seemed to bring a different mentality was something unique. There just might be something special to it.

"Make sure you guys get into the training room and get the treatment you need but don't be late for dinner. Remember to study your scouting reports and get some rest tonight. We have a big game tomorrow."

"Yes, sir!" the 12 players seemed to say in unison.

A little more than 24 hours later as the Eagles sat down next to their lockers after finishing up with their rivals, they weren't quite sure what Coach was going to say.

"Last time we met after a game, I was frustrated and didn't know if there was any hope to the season. Tonight, I'm frustrated but I'm extremely hopeful."

Coach Dunn took a sip of water and continued.

"I'm frustrated because you guys fought your tails off tonight. I wanted to see you get the 'W'. That probably would have been too much like a movie. But make no mistake. All those things you guys talked about were real. You might not have gotten rewarded on the scoreboard for the new attitude, but it was obvious to anyone watching that there was something different about you."

Coach Dunn could tell that they were glad he was recognizing them but still disappointed that they lost.

"You didn't win tonight on the scoreboard, but you won in my book. I know that might sound cheesy, but the truth is that you nearly beat an extremely good Tiger team tonight. You nearly pulled off the upset even though you hadn't built up habits throughout the course of the season. Imagine what can be done if we continue what we started the last couple of days. The good news is we have enough time left in the season to develop the kind of habits on the court that will match your attitudes."

Coach Dunn picked up a dry erase marker and approached the white board, writing the word LEADERSHIP.

"This is what I saw tonight. I saw leadership. I saw teammates helping each other. I saw unselfish play. And near the end when it was apparent that we weren't going to win, I didn't detect any finger-pointing or blame being thrown around. I saw leadership from 12 guys, not just a senior or a starter or from a coach. As I said I'm hopeful because I'm seeing genuine leadership from you guys."

Coach Dunn paused and looked at the white board. He pointed at the word LEADERSHIP and then pointed at each one of his players saying their name out loud.

"Each of you can be a positive leader for us moving forward. This can still be a special season because, as you've already discovered, you are interconnected and responsible to one another on this journey. And make no mistake, it is a journey, not just a destination. You didn't win tonight but you took a giant step forward on this journey together. Now, bring it in."

The players got up from their seats quickly and met in the center of the locker room.

With an enthusiasm unmatched at any point in the season, the team said together "1, 2, 3, TEAM."

TOURNAMENT

The change in mentality continued and new habits were developed as the Eagles finished the regular season on a nine-game winning streak. Furthermore, those 12 guys ended up going deeper in the playoffs than any previous Eagles team had in school history.

After the final buzzer had sounded ending their amazing playoff run, the players walked to the locker room. Coach Dunn addressed this group one last time and then let the seniors say a few words.

Doing his best to hold back his emotions, Brandon spoke first.

"It seems like only yesterday I was a freshman. I can't believe it's done. I thought I'd win plenty of championships."

Brandon took a deep breath.

"Obviously we didn't win any championships during my four years. But I can honestly say that what we accomplished this year after starting out as we did may have been more satisfying than winning any trophy. I will never forget the way we came together during this journey."

He couldn't believe that the season, and his basketball career, was finished, but he had a sense of peace in knowing that he did what he could for the program.

"I'm so proud of you guys. I never wanted a season to continue more than I wanted this season to continue. Not because of the whole 'survive and advance' thing we all want at tournament time but because you guys are my family. We grew together this year and that is something I'll never forget. Thanks, guys!"

Learie then stood up and walked to the whiteboard on the wall.

"Until we had that team meeting, I never liked these things," he said pointing at the whiteboard.

"These boards were just something Coach would scribble on and write about things that I didn't really care about. That bus trip. That meeting the next day. That stuff changed my life. I know you don't expect me to be this deep, but it was about more than basketball for me."

Learie took off his wristband and repeatedly stretched it out in front of his teammates.

"This little thing reminds me every day that those ten things we learned on that bus trip and in that meeting are things that we can do no matter how much talent we have as a basketball player, or in life, for that matter. I can apply all of those things to being a student, to being an employee one day, to being a husband, or a father."

Antonio interrupted Learie, "Wait, is there something you haven't told us?"

"Come on, man! I was pouring my heart out to you and you have to go and make a joke."

"You're right. My bad!"

Rolling his eyes and shaking his head, Learie continued.

"Anyway, I'm a better man, not just a basketball player, because I realized that I can display leadership in all aspects of my life. I can do those ten things in all areas of my life. Thanks for helping me see that."

As Learie approached his seat, Coach Dunn walked over to him and gave him a big hug.

"I'm so proud of you. I never thought I'd be saying this to you, but you were key to us making this tournament run. We're going to really miss you next year."

"Coach, you're going to make me cry. Stop that," said Learie.

Coach Dunn released his grip on Learie, but he wasn't quite finished with his praise.

"Your stats might not win you a place in the record books, but we'll be talking about your legacy for quite a while. Thanks for stepping up and taking responsibility."

From the corner of the locker room, Jaylen nudged forward on his crutches.

"I know that I'm not a senior, but I wanted to quickly say something."

As one of the most respected people, not just on the team, but on the entire campus, all eyes were now on Jaylen.

"I think I speak for the entire team when I say to the captains, thank you for showing us a great example of leadership and helping inspire us all to not only be good followers but to step up and be leaders ourselves."

Brandon and Learie nodded. They were appreciative of Jaylen and his words. He was already a positive leader and next year, he'd make a good team captain.

"As for you, Coach, thanks for trusting us enough and empowering us to develop as leaders. We learned that we're all on this journey together."

Jaylen adjusted his weight on the crutches before continuing.

"I wish this season wasn't over, but the good news is our journey is still going on. I can't wait to have some recruits on campus and for them to see our culture and share with them the main thing that we're all about."

Coach Dunn looked at Jaylen, picked up a marker, and then wrote something on the whiteboard.

"That's exactly right, Coach. That's the word. That's what we're all about. LEADERSHIP."

the
CAPTAIN

SUMMER
2020

For more information
and a free gift, please visit ...

TheCaptainBook.com

SUCCESS IS A CHOICE.
WE ALL CHOOSE TO BE BETTER!

1.) Lose the Excuses

2.) Excel in your Role

3.) Always be on time

4.) Display a good attitude

5.) Encourage team members

6.) Remain committed and focused

7.) Supply effort and energy

8.) Help and serve others

9.) Improve and be coachable

10.) Prepare to win

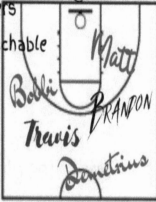

LEADERSHIP!

That's what
we're ALL about!

SUCCESS IS A CHOICE
WHAT CHOICE WILL YOU MAKE TODAY?

Interested in Jamy speaking at your event, working with your team, or conducting a workshop for your organization? You can connect with him at . . .

Linkedin: JamyBechler

Twitter: @CoachBechler

Website: JamyBechler.com

Instagram: @CoachBechler

Facebook: JamyBechlerLeadership

Email: speaking@JamyBechler.com

Other Books by Jamy Bechler

www.JamyBechler.com/Resources